SOMERSET TOWNS

CHANGING FORTUNES 800–1800

SOMERSET TOWNS

CHANGING FORTUNES 800–1800

TONY SCRASE

TEMPUS

To the memory of
my Aunt Daisy

First published 2005

Tempus Publishing Limited
The Mill, Brimscombe Port,
Stroud, Gloucestershire, GL5 2QG
www.tempus-publishing.com

British Library Cataloguing in Publication Data.
A catalogue record for this book is available from the British Library.

ISBN 0 7524 3423 3

Typesetting and origination by Tempus Publishing Limited
Printed in Great Britain

CONTENTS

ACKNOWLEDGEMENTS

My thanks are due to all of the following:

Paul Revell at the Faculty of the Built Environment, UWE for work on the maps and diagrams; Tina Hampson for work at the National Archives mainly on tax rolls in poor condition; Peter Fleming of the Humanities Faculty, UWE as two requests of his for me to speak at seminars set me on this particular course; Peter Kemmis Betty at Tempus Publishing; my cousin Jill Struthers for help with proof reading; and to the staff of the Somerset Record Office and the staff of the Somerset County Library's Local Studies Collection for their unfailingly helpful responses to all my requests.

Acknowledgements for illustrations are due to Professor Mick Aston for *11* and *60*; the Somerset Archaeological and Natural History Society for *23* and *29*; and the Somerset Archive and Record Service for *14*; and the British Library for the portion of Saxton's Map of Somerset reproduced on the cover.

Abbreviations

CUH	*Cambridge Urban History of Britain* series editor P. Clark, Cambridge University Press, 2000
	Volume I *600-1540* edited D.M. Palliser
	Volume II *1540-1840* edited P. Clark
CPR	*Calendar of Patent Rolls* HMSO, London, 1901–
HMC *Wells*	Historical Manuscripts Commission *Calendar of the Manuscripts of the Dean and Chapter of Wells* 2 volumes, HMSO, London, 1907 & 1914
OS	Ordnance Survey
PRO	The National Archives (until recently the Public Record Office)
SRO	Somerset Record Office
VCH	*Victoria County History of Somerset* Volumes I and II edited W. Page and Volume III onwards edited R.W. Dunning, Oxford University Press for the Institute of Historical Research, London
	Dates of publication: I in 1906, II in 1911, III in 1974, IV in 1978, V in 1985, VI in 1992 and VII in 1999
WTH	Wells Town Hall archives

CHAPTER I

INTRODUCTION

PURPOSE

This piece attempts to chart the changing fortunes of the towns of Somerset in the medieval and early modern periods. To set them in context statements in various parts of the *Cambridge Urban History of Britain* can be drawn together to suggest that *c.*1300 there were in England some 50 places of over 2,000 population and 660 market towns of between 300 and 2,000 persons (*CUH* i 2-3, 96-7, 274-5, 441-5, 506-9 & 747-70). This indicates a rather flat urban hierarchy with London at the top followed by the provincial capitals such as Bristol and Coventry; then came major regional centres (in the south-west, Exeter and Salisbury), larger market towns and, finally, the minor market towns of 300 to 1,000 population.

Relatively reliable statistics to set Somerset against this standard are only available with the 1377 poll tax. By that time famine and plague had cut populations back. For example, there were by then nationally only about 38 to 40 towns of more than 2,000. The Somerset figures therefore need to be interpreted accordingly. Nevertheless, it is clear from fig. 27 that Somerset was a county without any large towns. Apparently it had only market towns. Furthermore, places such as Nether Stowey and Ilchester were so small that their urban status must be in doubt.

There are a number of possible explanations for this situation. Was the south-west in some way different and a natural terrain for small towns? Alternately was Bristol such a vigorous neighbour that it inhibited growth within its sphere of influence? Or could it be a matter of too many landowners trying too hard to exploit the benefits offered by town foundation? It is hoped that the discussions which follow will throw some light on these questions as well as investigating the fortunes of the county's towns.

Inevitably such a study raises two further questions. Firstly, it focuses attention on available sources and their strengths and weaknesses. Secondly, it calls into question the issue of what constitutes a town. This is critical at the bottom of the hierarchy where the distinction between a town and a village with a market is difficult and where past commentators have produced different answers.

ORIGINS, DISTRIBUTION AND FOUNDERS

Archaeologists have found no eighth-century trading places in Somerset equivalent to *Hamwic* (Anglo-Saxon Southampton), *Lundunwic* or Ipswich further east. So our starting point must be the burghal hidage. This document of Edward the Elder's time lists places set up by his father, King Alfred, and probably by Edward himself to act as strong points against Viking incursions. Each was then allocated a number of hides of land. These seem to relate to the length of the ramparts and therefore are likely to have established the estates which had to provide a garrison. The places are a mixed group in several ways. Some were pre-existing settlements, some were new creations and others were reoccupied sites. As a result they include both former Roman towns and Iron Age hill forts. Somerset reflects this diversity.

The hidage lists five *burhs* in Somerset. They were Axbridge, Bath, Langport, Lyng and Watchet. There is general agreement that Lyng was a fort and never achieved any urban characteristics (Aston and Leech 1977 87-91: Aston 1984 183-5; Hill and Rumble 1996 209-11). It was the only *burh* in the county which never had a mint. Again the status of Watchet has been doubted and the modern consensus is that the site was Daws Castle, a reoccupied hill fort, rather than the subsequent port (*VCH* v 146; Costen 1992 136-9). All were relatively small sites well below the size of Exeter, Dorchester and Wareham which each exceeded 60 acres (24ha).

It should be noted that in Somerset there was a division of functions that were united in places further east, for example at Winchester and Canterbury. Here there was a *burh* at Axbridge while the centre for royal administration was at Cheddar and the minster church (or subsequently the cathedral) at Wells. Similarly, Langport was separated from the centre of the royal estate at Somerton while the minster church was probably at Northover (the north bank suburb of Ilchester). In each case the *burh* was to the west adjoining navigable water. As a result it had both the potential for trade and a defensive role to check any Viking movement up the river system. Later Wells and Somerton were to become towns and even Cheddar was more than an ordinary village with its large church, fair and sophisticated market cross. However, it would be going too far to assume that the initial division precluded large-scale development of the *burh*. This is demonstrated by Bristol, which emerged about a century later in a similar position in relation to the manor of King's Barton while the minster was in a third location at Westbury-on-Trym. Bristol also was to the west of the royal manor and adjoining navigable water. It was, of course, the major success in the south-west.

By the time of Domesday, Axbridge, Bath and Langport definitely had urban characteristics and had been joined by at least eight other places (Bruton, Crewkerne, Frome, Ilchester, Ilminster, Milborne Port, Milverton and Taunton, see *1* and *2*). However, Domesday is an unsatisfactory source for towns in Somerset, listing some places as having burgesses but no market and others a market but no burgesses (*1*). Indeed, only Langport and Bath are specifically described as boroughs although this status is implied at Taunton, as one of the customary dues is 'borough right'. As a result a number of other places have been suggested as towns (Dunning 1983 25 & 43; Bettey 1986 25). The most common are Yeovil and Wells. The former's claims are based mainly on an enigmatic entry in Domesday that to one of the two manors are added 22 plots which 22 men held jointly before 1066 and who pay 12s. Wells is claimed as a town on the basis of its cathedral and an ambitious street pattern orientated on the Anglo-Saxon cathedral rather than its successor (Aston 1984 177 & 193-4; Scrase 1989 19-24; Rodwell 2001 120-2). However, earlier suggestions that Somerton was an Anglo-Saxon town are now generally rejected (Aston 1984 186). It should also be mentioned that in the intervening period between the burghal hidage and Domesday South Cadbury had emerged as a *burh*. It was one of a number of creations that emerged as a response to the Danish attacks in the time of Ethelred II (or the Unready). The mint was shifted from Ilchester to the greater security of a hill fort just as Old Sarum replaced Wilton. However, South Cadbury did not develop any enduring urban characteristics in contrast to Old Sarum. This was despite the considerable efforts put into refurbishing the defences and building on the hill top (Alcock 1995 154-60).

At the opposite pole to the Domesday towns was Lyng. It was undoubtedly a small agricultural settlement. Similarly it is stated that Watchet had one slave, one smallholder, one plough and a mill. However, this may relate to a small private holding within the large royal manor of Williton. It is thus worth looking at the combined entry for the three large royal manors of Williton, Cannington and Carhampton. There is nothing clearly urban apparent, but as they had never paid tax it could be hidden. Even the number of hides in the manors was unknown. Also, under the entry for Old Cleeve is the statement that this manor had attached to it the third penny of borough right for Carhampton, Williton, Cannington and North Petherton. This obscure picture may be contrasted with a different form of evidence. As a mint Watchet was very active, being exceeded in coin production in this area only by Bath, Ilchester and Bristol (*1c*). Once again this needs to be put in context by a wider picture. All three were minor compared

a. by number of burgesses
1. Bath   186
2. Ilchester   109
3. Milborne Port   67
4. Taunton   64
5. Langport   34
6. Axbridge   32
7. Bruton   17

b. by yield of market
1. Ilchester   £11- 0s- 0d
2. Crewkerne   £4- 0s- 0d
3. Taunton   £2-10s- 0d
4. Frome   £2- 6s- 8d
5. Ilminster   £1- 0s- 0d
6. Milverton   10s- 0d
7. Milborne Port   not separately stated

c. by know Anglo-Saxon coins minted 973-1066
1. Bath*   476
2. Ilchester   379
3. Watchet   103
4. Taunton   79
5. Bruton   62
6. Crewkerne   29
7. South Cadbury   23
8. Langport*   23
9. Axbridge   16
10. Milborne Port   14
11. Frome (?)   6
12. South Petherton   4
* also minted before 973

d. Somerset mints in context

Exeter [8]	1,360
Bath [17]	476
Ilchester [19]	379
Shaftesbury [29]	307
Bristol [35]	246
Cricklade [44]	121
Watchet [46]	103
Malmesbury	99
Dorchester	95
Taunton	79
Bridport	37
Launeston	1

Sources Metcalf 1998 298-301 and for pre-973 coins Hill 1981 131-2. Figures in square brackets national rankings after *CUH* i 750-1. It is not certain that coins inscribed FRO are from Frome.

e. by percentage of known moneyers
1. Ilchester [25]
2. Bath [30]
- Bristol [33]
3. Taunton [51]
4. Watchet [59]
5. Axbridge [60]
6. Bruton [61]
7. South Cadbury [63]
8. Milborne Port [66]
9. Langport [68]
10. Crewkerne [71]
11. Frome [74]
12. South Petherton [80]

Figures in square brackets national rankings after Hill 1981 130. None of the places scored as much as 2% and South Petherton was below 0.1%.

1 Domesday towns ranked

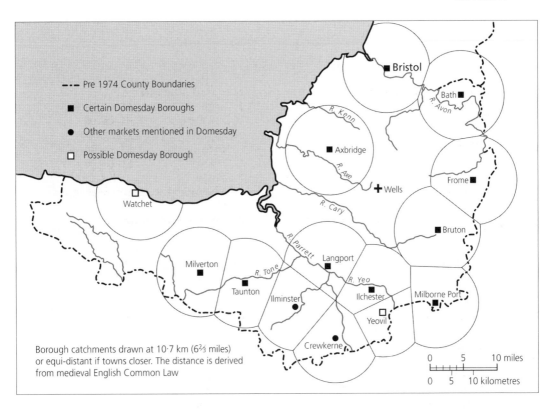

2 The Towns of Somerset at the time of the Domesday Survey

with London and Southwark's 10,758 known coins, York's 4,805, Winchester's 2,932 or Exeter's 1,360 (*CUH* i 750-1). However, there was a profusion of mints in Somerset with 12, as against seven in Wiltshire, four in each of Devon, Dorset and Gloucestershire and one in Cornwall (*3*). In addition four in the region are unidentified. The most active was probably in Devon. Archaeology has produced a total of four coins from the other three. Die-links tie one to Dorchester and the other two to Shaftesbury. Given that town's location in the north-east extremity of Dorset, it is possible that the missing sites were in Wiltshire or Somerset. Cross-border links are known. One of the more active Shaftesbury moneyers also worked at Milborne Port. Generally, the abundance of Somerset mints may again suggest a tendency towards the fragmentation of functions here (Metcalf 1998 238-48 and 296-301).

From all the evidence it seems that in 1086 Bath was the leading town in the county with Ilchester second and probably Taunton third with Milborne Port close behind. However, none of the 11 or so towns in Somerset was large by national standards. All are placed well down the lists Alan Dyer produced to try to evaluate pre-Conquest and Domesday towns (*CUH* i 748-53). This

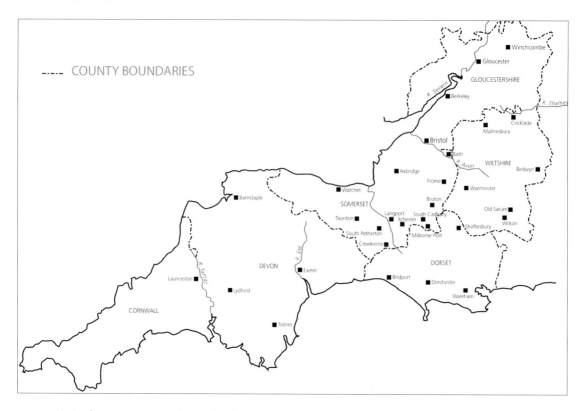

3 Anglo-Saxon mints in the South West

assessment can be confirmed by another form of evidence that he did not use. Important and prosperous towns of the late Saxon and early Norman period are often characterised by a profusion of churches including parish churches whose territory was limited to a few town blocks. Bath and Ilchester shows some signs of this. Bath had five churches besides the abbey while Ilchester had at least seven. These may seem excessive to us but hardly compare with Winchester's 54 parishes and a total of 69 places of worship. Norwich was similar while Lincoln and York each had nearly 50. Nearer to Somerset, Bristol had 18 parishes plus a variety of other religious houses. Bath and Ilchester were more comparable to Southampton which had five parish churches and Wareham which had seven including three with substantial territories beyond the walls. Of the other early Somerset towns only Taunton had more than one church and there one also served the priory.

This lack of a major town had a result in the post-Conquest period which sets Somerset apart. If one disregards the north-west, which was not yet fully incorporated into the English state and its shire system, and the two very small counties of Middlesex and Rutland, then Somerset is unique in a lack of royal castles imposed on its towns between 1066 and 1086. Generally William

I had castles built at the county town and any other of strategic importance, for example, at Stamford on the London–York road or at the major ports of Dover and Bristol. Drage characterised those places selected as centres of local administration possessing a large population and situated on an important route. It seems that none of the small towns of Somerset met all these criteria and that it was difficult then (as now) to rank them. Much of the county could, no doubt, be controlled from Bristol but the nearest royal garrisons to its southern and western parts were variously at Old Sarum, Dorchester, Exeter and Barnstaple (Drage 1987 117-21).

This absence would have had great short-term benefits. The Conqueror imposed his castles for military reasons and as symbols of the new regime. The local population were not considered and their suffering could be vast. Houses were usually destroyed. Numbers ranged from only eight at Wallingford rising through 27 at Cambridge and around 40 at Canterbury to 98 at Norwich and 166 at Lincoln, while at York one of the seven 'shires' (the administrative subdivisions of the Anglo-Danish city) was laid waste. It could be even worse. At Norwich a church was destroyed, its graveyard obliterated and its contents incorporated in the castle earthworks. Local people would have seen family remains disinterred. They may have been conscripted to do the work. In the longer term the castles could have benefits. As centres of justice and administration and the residence of somebody of wealth they often helped to confirm the dominance of the county town *(Ibid* 119-22; Scrase 2002b 36).

After the disruption of the Conquest came the great period of town foundation in the twelfth and thirteenth centuries. The result was a considerable expansion in the stock of towns and a number of failures from over-ambitious provision. The general view of the stock can be seen from the two volumes compiled for the purposes of rescue archaeology (Leech 1975; Aston and Leech 1977), from Aston's chapter in his and Burrow's *Archaeology of Somerset* (Aston and Burrow 1982) and from Dunning's *History of Somerset* (Dunning 1983). They are agreed, except that Aston in 1982 added Merryfield (or Merefield) in East Coker parish founded before 1275 but so transitory as to have left no physical remains (Aston & Burrow 1982 127-8), while Dunning adds the abortive foundation of Southwick opposite Langport but does not mention Merryfield. Bettey subsequently took a slightly different line with a list headed 'Medieval Boroughs'. As this title indicates he followed Beresford and Finberg and used the existence of burgage tenure as the defining characteristic. As a result he omits Crewkerne and Frome from amongst the Anglo-Saxon creations, Southwick from amongst the abortive foundations and all of Castle Cary, Dulverton, Glastonbury, Ilminster, Keynsham, Minehead, Pensford and Wincanton from the other three's common ground. However, he does mention some of these as towns elsewhere. In fact several feature on the map of 'Medieval New Towns' opposite the table emphasising the need to attend to terminology. Also he includes Merryfield in his borough list. Finally, he includes the two elements on the south bank of the Avon at Bristol, that is Redcliffe and Temple Fee (Bettey 1986 48-9; Beresford and Finberg 1973). It should be pointed out that research for the *Victoria County History* has now established borough status and the existence of burgages at North Petherton (see below) and Wincanton (*VCH* vi 282-3 & vii 215).

All the places named by any of the above are considered here except for Redcliffe and Temple Fee. These are excluded because they were incorporated into Bristol by its 1373 charter and therefore lie outside our study area for much of the period covered. Moreover, prior to 1373 they are generally submerged in the large manor of Bedminster. The only separate mention was in 1327 when Temple Fee paid £2 6s 4d indicating a wealth of about £46 which would place it in the middle rank of Somerset towns between Somerton and Keynsham (see *17* and *18*).

However, a number of other places have a case for possible addition to the list. More recent research has revealed another attempt at town creation in West Pennard parish named, unimaginatively, New Town (pers. com. Dr R.W. Dunning). In addition, the dean and chapter of Wells attempted to promote a town at Congresbury (pers. com. R. Broomhead). It also had a fair although this was never of more than local significance (Hulbert 1936 106). Rather more long-term claims may be urged for North Petherton and South Petherton. As mentioned, the former definitely had a medieval borough and a market as the *Victoria County History* reveals (*VCH* vi 282-3). Also Leland described it as 'a praty uplandische towne' or, in the modern translation, an attractive country town (Toulmin Smith 1964 i 161; Chandler 1993 422). The status of South Petherton is also reasonably clear. Dunning mentioned it as a possible Anglo-Saxon town although it did not feature in his map of towns (Dunning 1983 25 and 43). Presumably his reference was occasioned by a short-lived mint. Then in 1213 King John either granted or confirmed its possession of a market and fair. It certainly had a market place and a market cross (*VCH* iv 172-3 & 188). Leland did not go that way but Gerard described it as a town with a little market which is similar to his categorisation of a number of places, including Dulverton and Minehead (Bates 1900 7, 12 & 115). Furthermore, both places feature in early modern lists of towns and were therefore included in the study of English small towns by the Centre for Urban History at Leicester University (Clark, Gaskin and Wilson 1989 ii-iii & 145-6). As a result they are included in fig. *4*.

The resultant distributions are interesting. According to the medieval lawyer Bracton, the Common Law rule was that markets should be at least 6 ⅔ miles (10.8km) apart although 10 miles would probably be more realistic (Steane 1984

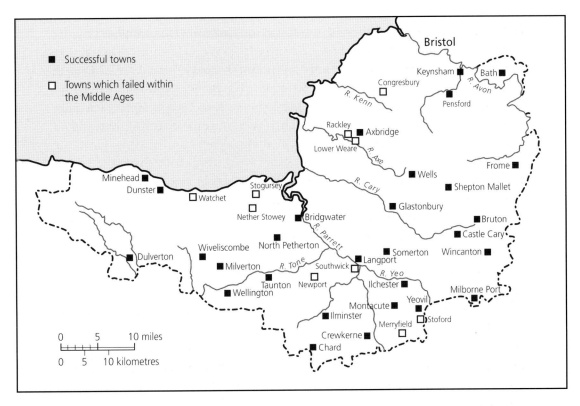

4 The Medieval Towns

126). Fig. *2* shows the Domesday towns with a 6⅔-mile radius or less where catchments overlap. The pattern shows that when Bristol is added the periphery of the county is well covered but in the centre Axbridge was isolated, leaving room for a number of further towns. Fig. *4* shows how that need was met and exceeded. No attempt to add catchments has been made as the result is too visually confusing. The only differentiation is to indicate which foundations were abortive or had failed within the Middle Ages. However, areas of over-provision are readily apparent. One group is in the south where Ilchester, Montacute, Milborne Port, Yeovil, Merryfield and Stoford are too close to each other and the situation is worsened when it is remembered that Sherbourne was just over the Dorset border between Yeovil and Milborne Port. Furthermore, the outer members of this cluster are also too close to other places: Ilchester to Langport and Somerton; Milborne Port to Wincanton; Merefield to Crewkerne; and Montacute to Ilminster, South Petherton and Crewkerne (see also *41*). There is also clustering between the Mendips and the Levels. Lower Weare and Rackley are far too close to each other and Axbridge. Further east Wells is less than 5 miles (8km) from both Glastonbury and Shepton Mallet. It is thus easy to see

15

why New Town (West Pennard) was a failure. Bruton, Wincanton and Castle Cary form a final over-close cluster.

There are also negative areas. Some have physical explanations. The higher areas of the west have few towns and they are mainly grouped around the area's fringe. Exmoor and the higher parts of the Blackdown, Brendon and Quantock Hills were obviously sparsely occupied and physically unwelcoming. The wetlands of the Levels and the high ground of the Mendips were also unsuitable. However, the lack of towns in the north of the county need some other explanation.

Part of the problem is the lack of research. This is well illustrated by *The Archaeology of Avon*. This has a section on towns in the chapter on Late Saxon Avon but it mainly deals with Bath and Bristol. Only in its last paragraph does it look elsewhere and then it is only to mention the Domesday market

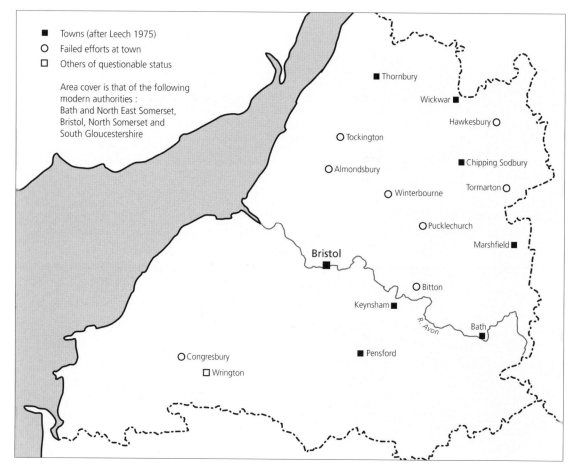

■ Towns (after Leech 1975)
O Failed efforts at town
□ Others of questionable status

Area cover is that of the following modern authorities :
Bath and North East Somerset, Bristol, North Somerset and South Gloucestershire

■ Thornbury
Wickwar ■
Hawkesbury O
O Tockington
■ Chipping Sodbury
O Almondsbury
Tormarton O
O Winterbourne
O Pucklechurch
Marshfield ■
Bristol
■
O Bitton
Keynsham ■
R. Avon
Bath ■
O Congresbury
■ Pensford
□ Wrington

5 Towns and abortive town foundations around Bristol

at Thornbury. Its cover of the High Middle Ages comprises a chapter each on Bristol and Bath supplemented by another on their mints. No other town gets more than a passing mention (Aston and Iles 1984 85-6, 115, 126 & 145-75). However, Leech and Dunning were agreed that only Bath, Keynsham and Pensford can be so ranked in the north Somerset area. An obvious explanation for this sparse pattern is the dominance of Bristol. It was so important that lesser places could not make headway close to it. To add to the problem, Bath was so well established by 1086 that it compounded the difficulties for town founders. To test this assertion it is useful to look at the northern side of Bristol. Fig. 5 shows the places covered in Leech's study of the small towns of the Avon area (Leech 1975). It is apparent that there is a wide belt around Bristol without towns. Thornbury and Chipping Sodbury are both just over 10 miles (16km) from the historic core

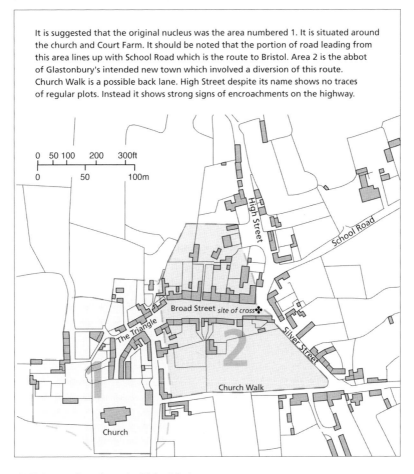

6 Wrington (based on the Tithe Map)

7 Wrington. The buildings in Broad Street form a group, giving the air of a market place. The cross stood at the far end by the public house

and Marshfield over 12 miles (19km). The impact of Bristol is reinforced by the addition to Leech's towns of the various failed towns shown by Smith and Ralph (Smith and Ralph 1972 43). In contrast, less is known of the Somerset side but one must suspect that further detailed research will find abortive foundations to match those of Gloucestershire. Congresbury, mentioned above, is one example. Another place deserving attention is Wrington. It has a very urban-looking central square, as figs 6 and 7 show. This square was embellished with a market cross until the eighteenth century and Wrington had a fair (Hulbert 1936 106). Also it was another place to feature as a town in early modern lists and was therefore included in the Centre for Urban History's statistics.

Given the strength of the Bristol market and the resilience of Bath, one might question the status of Keynsham and Pensford. The former was probably sustained by the needs of its abbey and by its position as a crossing place on the rivers Avon and Chew. As we shall see it declined sharply after the Dissolution. Pensford is more of a mystery. It is somewhat further from Bath and Bristol (about 8 miles or 13km from each) and had the next bridge over the Chew. Also the river here was suitable as a power source. It was exploited for the cloth industry as Leland remarked and later for metalworking. Nevertheless, it was a small place and possibly at the bottom of the urban hierarchy. Alternatively, it may be an example of something rather different. Other small places with some urban characteristics, notably Norton St Philip, will be mentioned as arguments develop below and the matter will be returned to in Chapter 5.

The question of who founded these towns is significant. However, the evidence is often lacking. Thus the first we know of Downend is that Philip de Columbers owed 10s for *burghrit* (that is the right to hold a *burh*) in 1159 (Aston and Leech 1977 89). Whether or not he was the founder is unclear. Similarly a number of places are first known as towns when they were permitted their own jury at the assizes. Even if there is a charter one must often wonder if it was actually regularising what was already there in a period when documentary evidence was becoming more important. The clearest case is Wells where the earliest charter (which does not survive) was *c.*1160. In contrast, in the latest review of the evidence Rodwell argues that there must have been market functions in Anglo-Saxon times and that the core plan also seems to be of that period (Rodwell 2001 120-3). So what follows is incomplete and may attribute foundation to a later period than the actual event.

The Anglo-Saxon towns were royal creations with the possible exceptions of Ilminster and Taunton. The market at Ilminster belonged to Muchelney Abbey. Taunton was originally built by King Ine of Wessex but destroyed soon after. It did not appear in the burghal hidage and was sold to the bishop of Winchester in 904 (Aston and Leech 1977 136). It only developed a market and mint after that date so the initiative was probably by the bishop. It is also striking that a number of later towns were the centres of royal manors in Anglo-Saxon times. Such places are referred to as royal vills or *villae regiae* in much of the literature. Here they were Keynsham, Milverton, North Petherton, Somerton and South Petherton. Only the town at Somerton was certainly a royal foundation but all were centres of estate and hundred administration which would have given them a size and range of functions that were appropriate for urban growth.

The other common nucleus for urban growth, both nationally and in the south-west, is held to be major ecclesiastical sites (*CUH* i 27-34 & 587-9). These might be monasteries or minster churches with a group of priests providing services for a large area. Obviously both would develop some central place functions. Unfortunately, it is difficult to apply this model in Somerset. To begin with the situation is unclear. The broad sequence of events may be reconstructed by combining the suggestions of Aston and Teresa Hall. The former argues that early monasteries in the area which would have belonged to the Celtic Church followed Egyptian and Levantine models transmitted via the island monastery of Lérins (off modern Cannes). In this system monks were taught in a central monastery but, having acquired the necessary self-discipline, moved on to life as a hermit. Thus the original centre may have been at Lantocai in Street with hermitages on Glastonbury Tor and the other islands of the Levels (Aston 1993 25 and 2002 36-41). Then, according to Hall, the incoming English authorities initially co-operated with pre-existing British institutions but grew suspicious of their orthodoxy due to controversy on the date of Easter, the tonsure and baptism. As a result these earlier establishments were resited and reformed. At the new locations roughly circular enclosures gave way to rectangular sites. Hermits' cells vanished as they did not fit the concepts of discipline in the Roman Church. As a result Lantocai was replaced by the lower site at Glastonbury. Simultaneously, at the end of the seventh and beginning of the eighth centuries a system of minster churches were put in place (Hall 2000 & 2002).

So we have an early phase of disruption. To add to our difficulties it is far from clear as to what were the subsequent minster churches. Thus Aston, having discussed Glastonbury, Congresbury and Cannington went on, 'there are numerous other places in the county which have some claim to having been minsters in the pre-Norman Conquest period' (Aston 2002 45). Costen calculated that there were over 20 places with claims to minster status in the county based variously on documentary, field archaeology, architectural and place name evidence (Costen 1992 145 & 153-7). Hase identified 29 as certain, likely or possible (Hase 1994 53). Part of the difficulty of identification probably stems from two problems. The first concerns actual terms. The Anglo-Saxons called monasteries 'minsters'. So there is both a linguistic and a functional overlap between monasteries and minsters in the sense of a preaching church serving a substantial area. Secondly, in national terms the system was certainly abused. Landowners established minsters to gain the advantages of 'bookland', that is land held by written grant in a royal charter and so exempt from many of the duties and dues of customary tenure. Also, foundations were used to provide a career for members of the founder's family. This could mean that the head of the house continued a lifestyle more appropriate to a secular hall. Bede attacked such abuses (Heighway 1987 98-101). Such dubious foundations may have helped to confuse the picture in Somerset by occasioning transitory references.

The picture is unclear in its detail. Nevertheless, the situation seems to have been similar to that with mints involving both fluidity and fragmentation. As a result it is difficult to discuss any impact on the growth of Anglo-Saxon or subsequent urbanism. Sites to be considered from the early (British) phase could include Cannington, Cheddar, Congresbury and Porlock, all of which became more than simple medieval villages but (as we shall see) failed to develop full urban functions. Also it is worth noting Aston's statement that 'it looks as if Dulverton may have been an important if as yet unappreciated ecclesiastical centre on the south side of Exmoor before it became a medieval town' (Aston 2002 38). Moving on to the minsters, Wells obviously started in this way but otherwise one can only say it was probably a contributory element at Crewkerne, Ilminster, Milborne Port and Taunton, while it may have had a role at Bruton, Keynsham, Milverton and Yeovil (Aston 2002 45; Hall 2002 53). However, the role of these ecclesiastical institutions before 1100 should not be overstated. As we have seen, the early development at Wells is problematic and wealthy Glastonbury shows no obvious signs of urban functions in Domesday although the editors of the most recent edition chose (unusually) to translate the original *villa* as 'town' (Thorn & Thorn 1980 90a). At Bath it is likely that both the abbey and *burh* status were attracted by site advantages – notably the focus of routes and the Roman walls – rather than having a more direct relationship to each other.

Later the Church was more active, as after 1100 the most prolific founders were the bishops of successively Bath and then Bath and Wells. They alone might be accused of trying rather too hard. Of their creations Wells was a success but Newport, Southwick and Rackley were failures. Wiveliscombe was never more than a small place and Chard and Wellington were very modest in the fourteenth century, although they improved in the longer term.

Most other towns were single efforts. Only Glastonbury managed two or three places depending on our assumptions. The first is that Shepton Mallet was the abbey's creation, as it was granted its weekly market in 1235 before it passed to the Mallet family. The second is that the abbot was intending to found a town at Wrington when he obtained a charter for both the fair and market from Edward II (Collinson 1791 i 206). In fact the monastic houses in Somerset seemed little concerned with town creation in contrast with, for example, the Benedictine houses in the West Midlands (Slater 1996 70-86). Apart from Glastonbury's efforts, Keynsham Abbey was presumably responsible for Keynsham and Muchelney founded Ilminster. The dean and chapter of Wells tried at Congresbury and may have had a role at Newport as they owned the manor. All other known foundations were by lay lords. Furthermore, apart from the count of Mortrain at Montacute all were men of regional or local significance only, for example William de Brewer at Bridgwater, the Mohuns at Dunster, the Gournays at Weare and the de Courcys at Stogursey.

How does this compare with other counties of the south-west? Wiltshire is closest to Somerset. In Domesday it had a total of 10 places with some urban characteristics, although variously described as borough, possessing burgesses or having a market. As we have seen, Somerset had 11 such places. The other three counties had appreciably fewer with Cornwall at the opposite pole with only one, Bodmin. So Cornwall had to struggle to catch up and by 1300 the earl of Cornwall had founded 10 boroughs in the shire plus Bradninch in Devon. As Slater remarked, this was exceptional for the region. The earl of Devon was the only other secular lord to exceed two or three creations (*CUH* i 597). In Gloucestershire, which lacked a resident bishop, all the towns except the Anglo-Saxon foundations of Gloucester, Bristol, Berkeley and Winchcombe were individual efforts. The lack of major monastic interest has already been mentioned. So if Somerset is distinct it is in the early level of royal activity, which sets it apart from three of its neighbours but not from Wiltshire.

This characteristic of Somerset and Wiltshire caught Hill's attention. He began by discounting two possible explanations. Firstly, there was Dolley and Metcalfe's tentative suggestion that the later West Saxon kings were no longer able to spend the greater part of the year in the old royal demesne (Dolley & Metcalfe 1961 148-9). There was therefore a small but constant need for coin to cover commuted food rents. Hill was able to show that in the mid-tenth century the king spent more time in Somerset and Wiltshire than anywhere else. Secondly, there was the possibility that the concentration reflected density of population and therefore demand for mints and markets. Using the statistics contained within the Domesday Book he was able to show that other shires had comparable densities of population. If it were a simple correlation with population East Anglia, for example, should have had as many small towns as Somerset and Wiltshire. Instead he suggested that this was deliberate policy by the king, who was seeking to restore his income in areas where grants to the church had seriously reduced his revenues (Hill 1978 218-22). This theory is consistent with another fact. In Somerset and Wiltshire the king kept the profits of justice in his own hands. Elsewhere he generally shared it with the earl, who had a third in contrast to the royal two-thirds. In some places the profits had been entirely granted away.

DOCUMENTARY SOURCES

The best sources for comparative study of all these towns and failed towns are found in the government's attempts to tax them. The more comprehensive survivals also allow Somerset to be set in national and regional contexts. As a result much of what follows will be concerned with the taxes listed below.

The 1327 Lay Subsidy

This is a nearly complete and undamaged record for Somerset although it is not so well-preserved universally. The Somerset lists include all certain towns but a number of remote places such as Stogumber and its neighbour Monksilver do not appear. However, it is quite likely that they are included in other units in the locality. The returns are daunting in their bulk. The Somerset records have over 10,000 names. So it has not been studied in totality for national comparisons. The Somerset material has been available in published form for over a century as it occupies the larger part of the Somerset Record Society's third volume (Dickinson 1899). Also the Worcestershire returns had been published slightly before allowing some comparisons (Eld 1895).

The 1334 Lay Subsidy

This subsidy became the basis of all later medieval subsidies and therefore survives well and gives general cover. It thus allows the most complete listing for Somerset and the opportunity for wider comparisons on wealth. The whole has been published (Glasscock 1975 for Somerset 258-75).

The 1377 Poll Tax

This is the best source for medieval population although it only gives a picture after the first plague outbreaks. Unfortunately, the full Somerset lists have never been published or closely analysed. Nationally the lists have been studied several times to produce lists of up to the top 100 towns (*CUH* i 758-60). As a result the four largest Somerset towns can be placed in a wider context. Also some of the other totals are available as a result of Russell's statistical analyses and these have been used in local studies. As a result the size of some of the smaller places can be given (Russell 1948 141-2 & 252; Dunning 1974 10-3). Many of the other records (PRO E179/169/34 & 35) seem in poor condition so that a major effort will be required to expand the list given in fig. *27*.

The 1524-5 Lay Subsidies

This was a break from the system and sums of 1334. It thus gives a much needed revision and a more widely based view of wealth. Wolsey's approach was subtle. In 1522 he organised a thorough assessment of wealth under the guise of a muster. It was to discover the rate at which all men should be assessed to be furnished with harness (that is armour). He promised (falsely of course) that the records would be burnt. Instead the information was used to extract a forced loan from the larger taxpayers. This was described as an 'anticipation'. Then in 1523 an Act authorised subsidies in 1524 and 1525. This was to be levied on the best of movable goods, rents from land or wages. The exemption limit was only £1. Again, with the exception of Bath for both 1524 and 1525 and Wiveliscombe for 1525 (Green 1889b; Hancock 1911 257-9), the Somerset material has not been published but it has been worked for national rankings. As a result the top five towns for both wealth and taxpaying population can be set in a wider context (*CUH* i 761-7). The reason for the neglect of the Somerset material was explained by Stoate. Many of the rolls are in poor condition as regards legibility. Five hundreds are missing and only 29 out of a total of 40 are reasonably legible (Howard and Stoate 1975 xii–xiii). To illustrate his point half of the membrane for Bruton hundred is missing, destroyed or illegible due to water damage (PRO E179/169/174). So a satisfactory county series is impossible.

The 1558 and 1581-2 Lay Subsidies
These have only recently been published. The 1558 records are very incomplete (Webb 2002 1-24). However, they do cover Castle Cary which is missing from the surviving documents for 1581-2. These latter records are far more complete and give a valuable picture for Somerset (Webb 2002 25-183 and 188-91).

The 1641 Lay Subsidy and Poll Tax and the 1642 Assessment
None of these three tax assessments survives in more than a very partial form but together they give a useful picture. Their combined value is enhanced when they are used with the comprehensive records of the male population provided by the Protestation returns of 1642 although these are also incomplete. Fortunately, the whole group has been published although the work is now hard to come by (Howard and Stoate 1975).

These sources raise a number of questions in interpretation. To begin with there is the standard problem encountered when working with tax records. It is whether observed changes show real alterations in wealth or population or instead reflect changes in the behaviour of one or more of government, the tax assessors, the tax collectors and the taxpayers. The classical case is the contrast between the 1377 poll tax and its successors. Apparent populations crumbled. Thus Bath had in 1377 some 570 payers but by 1379 this had fallen to 328 (Green 1889a) and was only 297 in the final collection of 1381 (Russell 1948 142). This might seem to imply a fall of population from 1,040 first to 656 and finally to 594. Similarly, Wells would appear to have declined from 1,802 inhabitants in 1377 to 974 in 1381. However, this was not due to a major recurrence of plague but to an interplay of actions by each of the parties involved. In 1379 and 1381 the government altered the rules. It adjusted the minimum age for payment but more importantly it increased the rates. In 1377 everybody paid 4d. In 1379 a graduated element was added so that the affluent paid more, peaking at £40 for a duke. Finally in 1381 it increased the base rate to 1s. Evasion of a tax tends to increase as people become accustomed to it and develop strategies of avoidance. Such reactions were intensified by the increases in what was levied. The approach of assessors seems to have been balanced by a mass exodus of those who did not intend to pay. Finally, there was, probably, a reluctance by collectors to insist, particularly as

In taxable goods (known properties in brackets)	In property (tax paid in brackets)
Paying £1	**9 properties**
Peter le Botoyr (1)	Thomas Testwode (£1)
Nicholas Camberlyn (0)	
Thomas Testwode (9)	**7 properties**
	Thomas le Devenische (2s)
Paying 10s	
Adam Cheleworth (5)	**6 properties**
Thomas Mason (1)	Thomas le Saltare (5s)
Richard Tholy (1)	
	5 properties
Paying 8s	Adam Cheleworth (10s)
Richard le Eyr (3)	Hugh de Somerton (5s)
Paying 5s	**4 properties**
William de Aystone (0)	Juliana le Kynge (-)
Thomas le Saltare (6)	Richard atte More (1s)
Hugh de Somerton (5)	William atte Putte (1s)
William atte Watere (2)	Walter de Strete (2s)
Stephen Wedmore (1)	
Paying 4s-6d	**3 properties**
Robert de Mertoke (3)	Gilbert Boghiare (1s)
	Richard Corteys, senior (4s)
Paying 4s	Richard Courteys, junior (1s)
Richard Courteys, senior (3)	Richard le Eyr (8s)
John Markaunt (2)	William le Ferrour (2s)
Thomas de Mertoke (2)	Robert de Mertoke (4s-6d)

8 Wells in 1327, wealth in taxed movables and land compared

the tensions that led to the Peasants Revolt became more and more apparent.

Next it must be remembered that these are lay subsidies, so that the church is not covered. So the total wealth flowing into Wells and, before 1539, into the monastic towns is not reflected. This is significant as all these institutions drew income from a wider area. It would be unrealistic to expect it all to be spent locally. Christopher Dyer's study of the West Midlands shows how ecclesiastic expenditure spread over a wide territory, with major dignitaries such as abbots and bishops looking to London, Coventry or Bristol for their needs (C. Dyer 1998 66-71). Nevertheless, part at least was spent in the town augmenting trade and employment, particularly in the building industry and for servants, grooms, laundresses and the like. This effect must have been most pronounced at

Glastonbury. At Domesday it had an income of £830 according to Holdsworth, which put it ahead of all other monastic houses and was exceeded only by the dioceses of Canterbury and London. In turn these three had incomes comparable with Corbett's Class A for lay lords, a group of the eight most affluent noblemen (Corbett 1926 509-10; Holdsworth 1995 38-9). By 1535 Glastonbury, like Westminster, enjoyed an income of about £4,000 per annum. This put them at the top of any table of religious wealth in Britain. The bishop and chapter at Wells together received an income of £2,573 per annum. For comparison the Crown estates yielded about £40,000 at that time (Hoskins 1976 53 & 126).

Also of prime importance is the question of what is being taxed. Medieval lay subsidies were levied on movables only. It was thus possible to minimise tax liability by investing in land. Figure *8* contrasts the wealth revealed by the 1327 subsidy and contemporary property holdings in Wells. The two are strikingly different. So medieval subsidies do not reveal the whole picture. In 1524-5 the government tried to break away from that system and the amounts set in 1334. The new system taxed the higher yielding of goods, rental income from land or wages. As fig. *30* shows, this succeeded in dramatically expanding the taxpaying population. The subsequent Tudor and Stuart taxes were levied, in effect, on goods or land. There might be occasionally a theoretical liability on wages but the threshold was so high that it does not affect the Somerset returns. To understand and compare these later subsidies, allowance has to be made for the fact that thresholds and rates varied both in time and between goods and land. So payment on apparently similar town wealth would vary dependant on the exact balance between the two elements. Also at times aliens and recusants were charged at higher rates or paid a poll tax if below the tax threshold.

Next one must consider the accuracy of the assessments. This was done locally. Before 1334 this was undertaken in towns by the more prominent and reliable citizens, in other words by the elite. The 1334 system left it to the inhabitants of the individual place to divide up the allocated sum. As government had opted out we have no records. Under the Tudors and Stuarts methods were formalised. Commissioners for each county were appointed by the Lord Chancellor and set out in the Act. Generally, they comprised JPs or country gentlemen of good standing. They in turn appointed high collectors and local assessors. These latter persons had the power to summons anybody before them and determine the value of their holdings. Actual collection was done by sub-collectors (often local constables) and delivered to the high collectors (Howard and Stoate 1975 v-vi; Webb 2002 vii-xix).

Obviously the assessors would want to maintain good relations with their neighbours and to restrict their own burden. As a result it is agreed that wealth was generally under-assessed. At the least sums were rounded down. For example it is obviously unlikely that the three richest burgesses of Wells in 1327 would each have had goods worth just £20 to justify their payment of £1 each. Similarly, the rich and influential were able to minimise their burden. In the Middle Ages the aristocracy and landed classes owed their position to landholdings so a system of tax on movables shifted most of the liability to the richer peasants, merchants and traders. Subsequently the landed classes used their position as commissioners and the technicalities of different rates to reduce their payments (Webb 2002 viii–ix).

The towns were not without influence despite the make-up of the commissioners. In 1581–2 they included Bishop Berkeley who had obvious links to Wells and Sir Maurice Berkeley who was in effect the proprietor of Bruton. Again one of the three high collectors was William Clark who had a Wells estate and was taxed there although his country house was at the former nunnery at Barrow Gurney (Webb 2002 xii–xvi). By 1641–2 the urban links had increased. Commissioners with Wells connections included: William Bull, whose father had been a Wells woollen draper with sufficient resources to set up as a country gentleman and who retained property interests there; Sir Francis Dodington whose brother-in-law was William Coward of Wells; George Powlett who owned property in the town; and Edward Weekes who had a house on the Liberty. Similarly Sir Charles Berkeley (Sir Maurice's third successor) would have continued to have a care for Bruton while in 1642 the mayor of Bath and an alderman were added to the list.

Given all this it is obvious that wealth is always understated and that the most affluent were able to depress their contributions. Allowing for this, assessments within a town were probably reasonable equitable. Comparisons between towns are less certain. As we shall see, conventions seemed to vary from place to place. However, these sources are all we have so they must be used but with appropriate caution.

There is a further set of problems with the unit used for the tax assessment. If it is drawn too tight, part of the town may be omitted. In Somerset this is most acute at Wells where the city had three units: the borough, the Liberty of St Andrew around the cathedral and the suburb of medieval Byestewalles or early modern East Wells. Only the first is always covered. It is unclear whether laymen living in the Liberty were included until they were specifically mentioned. This occurs, although perhaps partially, in 1524 when the town's returns end with an item headed Canon Barne, which was the name for the dean and chapter's manor. It lists 16 persons who all paid on wages and that is some 30 per cent of all the town's payers on wages. Only one of them paid more than the minimum 4d. The Liberty is actually named in 1581 when five people are listed, four paying on land and one on goods and three described as gentlemen. In contrast, East

Wells was never included. Furthermore, it is not separately listed elsewhere so that corrections can be made. It either appears as part of the large out parish of St Cuthbert's or, if the out parish is subdivided, as part of a tithing that also includes the hamlets of East and West Horrington. So all that follows understates the total wealth and population of Wells. Ilchester also had a suburb, Northover, which included the site of the early modern gaol (see *19*). However, Northover was a separate parish. As a result its returns are usually available and have been included with all the statistics for Ilchester set out below except those for 1548.

In Somerset the more common problem is of overlarge units. Many towns were set in large parishes. Occasionally, the returns make a distinction. Thus Chard borough is always listed separately from Chard lands and Milverton borough from the 'manor and denizen'. Also the early modern returns do begin to indicate some residents of hamlets in the larger parish. Thus in 1581-2 some payers in Dulverton are identified as of Ashway, Marsh and other places while in 1641 several Ilminster payers were described as of Sea, Horton, etc. All such persons have been excluded from the statistics presented here. But in most cases we lack this help and some judgement is involved.

Glastonbury is the most extreme example. Medieval returns are made not for the parish but for a larger unit known as Glastonbury 12 hides. This included Meare, Panborough and Godney. To include the 1327 and 1334 returns would thus inflate Glastonbury's size and affluence. As a result it is only listed from 1524-5.

Turning to parishes, the most problematic was Wiveliscombe. It has a large upland parish and in the period 1309-29 was said to have 31 burgages paying a shilling each (Aston and Leech 1977 159). But in 1327 it had 68 taxpayers, a number exceeded only by Frome amongst the county's towns. This would imply over two payers per burgage if they were all living in the town. For comparison Stogursey had 60 burgages in 1307 (*VCH* vi 132) and Wells over 300 in this period (Scrase 1993 9-74). These involve a ratio of four to five burgages to the taxpayer. Thus it is likely that many payers at Wiveliscombe were from outside the town. Indeed, it is possible that the borough formed only part of the main settlement. The port reeve was elected out of the part of the town called the 'Borough' (Aston and Leech 1977 159). To compound the difficulties the 1581 returns are for Wiveliscombe and Fitzhead. The editor helpfully has indicated those who can be identified from a 1580 court roll of Fitzhead (Webb 2002 128), but that cannot be taken as exhaustive. As a result Wiveliscombe is omitted from most of the tables.

For broadly similar reasons Congresbury and Wrington have been excluded. Both were large, rich parishes and any urban nucleus has not been certainly identified but presumably would have been small. Figure *6* shows that the nucleus of Wrington was still very small at the time of the Tithe Map, 1838, when the parish population was approaching 1,500. Further study of that map reveals considerable numbers of houses spread along the lanes converging on the central settlement plus a series of hamlets, Lye Hole, Cowslip Green and Redhill, on the east of the parish (SRO T/ph/t). To include the parish return would seriously mislead. In 1327 Wrington was worth £182 and in 1334 this had fallen to £150. The equivalent figures for Congresbury are £123 and £93. Such wealth would put them amongst the county's best towns. As regards Wrington there is a further problem in that the 1581–2 returns are for Wrington and Burrington.

The next in difficulty is North Petherton. Its urban functions were always small and it was set in a large parish taking in the southern fringe of the Quantocks and an appreciable area of the Levels. By the time of the 1841 Tithe Map (*VCH* vi 280) it included a number of subsidiary settlements such as Woolmersdon, North Newton and Northmoor. Unfortunately, the subsidies do not identify any sub units in contrast to Ilminster, Dulverton or South Petherton. Its inclusion is marginal and is based on the hypothesis that the spread of settlement on to the Levels was an early modern phenomenon and that the early figures may reflect North Petherton proper.

So for completeness it should be noted that of the places appearing in the tables the following may all include a substantial rural element on at least some occasions: Dulverton, Crewkerne, Frome, Ilminster, Milborne Port, North Petherton, Shepton Mallet, Somerton, South Petherton, Stogursey, Watchet and Wellington. One of the great advantages of the 1642 Protestation returns is that it distinguishes between the town and the rest of the parish for a number of these places.

Pensford presents an entirely different problem. The settlement developed on both sides of the River Chew. The river here formed the boundary between Publow and Stanton Drew parishes. As a result, returns for Pensford are lost in those for these two. Pensford only tends to appear in documents less bound to standard administrative units. Notable examples are medieval levies on sacks of wool or subsequently on cloth and a late seventeenth-century survey of inns. When it does feature it seems to be remarkably prosperous. For example in the 1390s Pensford produced an astonishing average of 5,141 pieces of cloth per year compared with 4,845 at Frome and around 2,400 at Wells. Moreover, this production was in relatively few hands. Pensford sellers averaged 84.3 cloths a year and four of them almost equalled the entire production of Wells (Ponting 1957 26; Shaw 1993 82). Again in the inn survey Pensford had 20 beds which places it 27th in the county in that respect (see *51*). However, it had stabling for 102 horses which was exceeded in only ten places, all larger towns (Dunning 1983 84; PRO WO 30/48). It is also significant that both parishes established chapels of ease at Pensford during the Middle Ages, suggesting that both wished to enjoy their share of the profits of a thriving community. The surviving church,

St Thomas, was in Stanton Drew, while the chapel on the Publow side is only remembered in the name Chapel Barton (Leech 1975 46 & 48).

Apart from the Protestation returns there are few additional comparative sources from the early modern period. Of the sixteenth- and seventeenth-century diocesan surveys, only that of 1563 survives in part. That of 1603 is absent and for the so-called Compton census of 1676 (elsewhere generally the most useful) Bath and Wells returned only a total for the whole diocese. Similarly, the Hearth Tax returns are unhelpful in Somerset. One has either the list of payments or the exemption certificates, never both. The Centre for Urban History study warned against the pitfalls of using these individually, particularly the exemptions. The problems are well illustrated in their tables for Somerset. They show estimated populations wildly out of line with others for the same place and wide conflicts for the same place in successive assessments. Thus Crewkerne has 516 in 1664 based on payers and 2,755 in 1670 based on exemptions. In similar circumstances Ilminster has a range of 470 to 1,578 (Clark, Gaskin and Wilson 1989 vi and 141-4). As a result the Hearth Tax returns are not used here.

However, Leland is of considerable use. In this he can be distinguished from William Worcestre writing some 70 years earlier. Worcestre gives us distances between places, dimensions of churches and details of associated saints. Towns hardly feature as such (Harvey 1969 35, 127-9 & 289-99). In contrast, as will be explained in Chapter 3, Leland seems to have a concept of a hierarchy of towns. Also more immediately he gives a quick impression of the smaller places, for example when he characterises Pensford as 'a pratty [sic] market townlet occupied with clothing'. This telling word 'townlet' appears only in Toulmin Smith's older edition of Leland. Chandler modernises the section to 'a pleasant little clothmaking town' (Toulmin Smith 1964 v 103; Chandler 1993 429). As a result I have generally cited Chandler as the more accessible version but have used Toulmin Smith when it gives more immediacy to Leland's classification of a place. Also the seventeenth-century survey of inns provides a useful perspective as do the accounts of Gerard, Celia Fiennes and Defoe (PRO WO 30/48; Bates 1900; Morris 1949; Defoe 1948). The lists of Blome in his *Britannia* of 1673 and Adams with his *Index Villaris* of 1680 are vital in showing what directly concerned people regarded as towns in the second half of the seventeenth century. As a result they formed the basis for the study by the Centre for Urban History at Leicester University already referred to.

As there are no suitable eighteenth-century sources, the 1811 census is used as an end point. 1811 is preferred to 1801 as it is felt that any difficulties in the first ever British census had been overcome by a decade later.

9 Wells. An extract from Simes' bird's-eye plan of 1735, showing High Street and Market Place. Note the features swept away by eighteenth-century improvement. They comprise the middle row in High Street; the High Cross, which was one of the grandest in the county with a considerable spire topping its arched form; Bekynton's Conduit (partly hidden by the cross); and the hall which served as all of market, town and assize hall

TOWN FORM AS EVIDENCE

The actual form of towns as seen today or as revealed in early maps and pictures can tell us much about a place's fortunes. Obviously a town extension or the colonisation of the market place by small properties seems to indicate a buoyant economy and a resultant demand for more houses. However, there are as usual problems. To begin with, a town's morphology may reveal relative chronology but it will not give dates. This is particularly difficult with market-place colonisation because as we will see there were two great phases. The first ran on from the thirteenth to the fourteenth century and the second began as town fortunes revived after 1550 and continued into the seventeenth century. The patterns do not enable us to distinguish the period. Indeed in Wells the middle row in High Street was commenced in 1345 but reached its full extent in 1571-2 (*9*). Next these are matters of interpretation. For example the centre of Somerton has a rectangular market place and leading north from this Broad Street. The various structures on the market are obvious encroachments. In addition the block between Broad Street and the churchyard stands out, being characterised by small plot depth allowing little or no garden (*10*). This seems to indicate encroachment but was it on the street, the churchyard or a strip from each? Finally the meaning

10 Somerton. The tower and east end of St Michael's church show it to be predominantly of thirteenth- and fourteenth-century work rather than Perpendicular. To the right, note the gardenless rears of houses on Broad Street indicating that they were created by encroachment on the highway or the churchyard

11 Langport from the air. The higher part of the town is on the left with the long straight of Bow Street stretching across the lower ground to the river. Back River hugs the rears of the Bow Street burgages. Once it would have been lined with quays on the town side but now much of the bank is overgrown. The promontory nature of the town set in a loop of the River Parrett is clear. *Courtesy Professor Mick Aston*

of the patterns can be ambiguous. While the appearance of middle rows in wide streets and island blocks in market squares does often accord with growth, one can also conceive of part of a market place being built on because trade was poor and it was surplus. There is even more doubt if the road network is used for public buildings such as market houses, town or guild halls. Such schemes could represent an easy option for a town authority unwilling to sacrifice the rent of a burgage or unwilling to buy one. Again such public building may have little to do with economics but represent an assertion of power by the town. We will see this to be the case with the sixteenth-century market house at Bath and town hall in Wells.

So town form is best combined with documentary and archaeological evidence. Unfortunately the former varies sharply between towns. Archaeological investigation has everywhere been limited. Much of the town centres are protected from development by designations as listed buildings, scheduled monuments and conservation areas while the major development pressure has

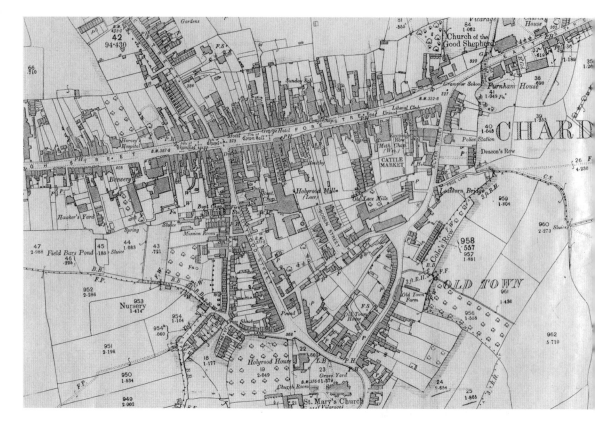

12   Chard. The second edition 1/2500 OS clearly shows the plan form. The original settlement lies to the south around the church. Bishop Joscelin's new town is to the north with a wide market street, regular plot depths and fairly standard frontages. Note also the sites of former buildings in the wide street and the way a number of burgage plots have been developed with rows of cottages such as Howard's Row. This last pattern is a sign of late eighteenth- and early nineteenth-century growth.

been for superstores sited at the edge of town away from the historic core. Most excavations in the heart of the towns have been small sites and it will take an accumulation of these to reveal any general trends.

To compound our difficulties, the plans of Somerset towns are rarely simple. Beginning with the Anglo-Saxon creations even their location is often in doubt. Non-urban Lyng is clear and Bath and Ilchester both presumably sheltered within the circuit of Roman walls. In contrast we have seen the doubts about Watchet. At Langport it is often assumed that the site was on the hill at the eastern end of the town where there are earthworks and a marked break in the slope. However, this has not yet been confirmed by excavation. Also it seems that Bow Street (which runs down to the bridge, *11*) is of Anglo-Saxon date and that the Back River was formed at the same time to give water access to the properties on its

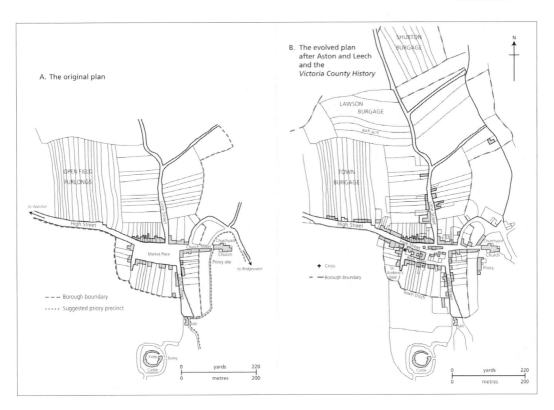

A. The original plan

B. The evolved plan
after Aston and Leech
and the
Victoria County History

13 Suggested evolution of the plan at Stogursey

south (*VCH* iii 16; Aston and Leech 1977 80-3: Aston 1984 181-3). At Axbridge Batt's suggestion of Moorland Street seems likely but there is again no evidence yet available to prove it (Batt 1973 22-3). So it seems that Axbridge and Lyng had a single street through a defended rectangle. However, they have a common topographic situation with most of the other places. They are what Aston (following Biddle) characterised as promontory sites. They have water, steep slopes or marshy ground on three sides with an easy approach from one direction only (Aston 1984 199-200). In contrast Bath was more ambitious although the loop of the River Avon means that it too can be described as a promontory. But within the walls it featured a rather crudely realised rectangular system although this was partly disguised by Bishop John de Villula's post-Conquest enlargement of the abbey and insertion of a bishop's palace. Originally the pattern was akin to that used at the *burhs* of Cricklade, Oxford, Wareham and Winchester (Biddle 1976 58-9; Cunliffe 1986 65-9). It confirms Bath's status in this early period.

When we move on to the creations of the High Middle Ages we find no ambitious gridiron schemes to rival those of Salisbury or New Winchelsea. As is typical nationally, most originated as what Beresford termed 'market based'

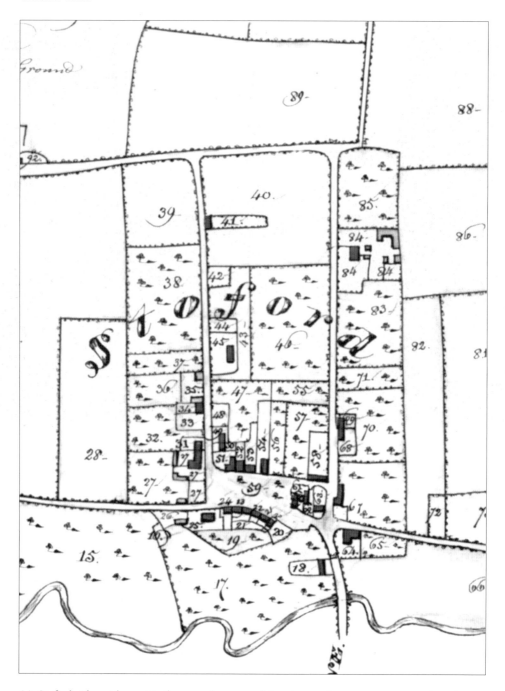

14 Stoford. The settlement in the second quarter of the nineteenth century as portrayed on the Barwick Tithe Map. By that time the former borough had shrunk to hamlet size but its planned rectilinear form and former market place (by this time a village green) are clear. Also a number of plots such as 54, 56 and 71 seem to preserve the dimensions of the original burgages. *Courtesy Somerset Archive and Record Service*

15 Shepton Mallet. The market place with its High Cross (a Victorian restoration but accurate as we have earlier pictures) and, on the right, a shambles, one of the permanent stalls which often formed an intermediate stage between a bench on market day and a middle row of shops with living accommodation over. These features survived because the market place was not a through route but a space off High Street.

patterns (Beresford 1967 153-6). These involved no more than laying out a market place and surrounding it by plots. The market place could be rectangular, a triangle set at a road junction or a wide main street. This involved minimum risk for the founder and could be extended if the new town flourished (Scrase 2002 25-31). Generally the most common pattern is the single street although these can vary in origins between a unified and coherent creation by a territorial lord intent on developing his estates to an aggregation of small initiatives by local occupiers (Slater 2003).

In Somerset these single street patterns are rare and only Chard (*12*) and Wellington conform to the type although this also seems to have been the intention at Newport. This contrasts with Gloucestershire where Chipping Camden, Chipping Sodbury, Marshfield, Moreton-in-Marsh, Newnham and

Wickwar provide classical examples of this pattern. Chard, Newport and Wellington were all founded by Bishop Joscelin early in the thirteenth century. Three other towns have fairly simple forms. Montacute seems to have started as a single street and then been enlarged by the addition of a second parallel street (Aston and Leech 1977 104-6). Stogursey in contrast began with a rectangular market which was surrounded by plots with perhaps a few extra on High Street and the roads towards the castle and church. It was then enlarged in two ways, by development on the tails of open field strips to both the north and west of the nucleus and by colonisation of the market square (*13*). Stoford's plan was rather more ambitious (*14*). It featured two parallel east–west streets. The more southerly was confined to the town area but the other led to the ford, giving a route into Dorset. These were crossed by one north–south road and the market place spanned their intersection. It had a little subsequent encroachment mainly by the guildhall but it is doubtful if the western end furthest from the market was ever occupied (Aston and Leech 1977 126-30).

All the other plans are composites showing signs of successive phases of development and varying levels of intervention by lords, major landowners and individual occupiers. Dunster is a reasonable example. In the north, High Street recalls classical single street patterns with a wide market street, regular plot depths and fairly regular frontages. To the south and west Church Street, Castle Hill and St George Street form a more complicated branching pattern with the possibility of highway encroachment where they meet. South of this, West Street and Water Street may be single street extensions but there is a more amorphous area around their junction and uniform plot depth is found only on the side towards the castle. The only exception to this mixed form is Pensford which shows no signs of any overall scheme and was probably created by individual occupiers along the road and riverside. This vigorous activity seems to indicate a period of growth and optimism across Somerset. This impression is strengthened by the fact that signs of middle rows or island blocks can be found in every town except Ilchester, Keynsham, Milverton, Montacute, North Petherton, Pensford, Wiveliscombe and Wrington. We have already seen how several of these were marginal in status. We shall see how others such as Ilchester and Montacute came to suffer severe economic difficulties.

Also it is possible to say something of phases of development in some towns. Taunton seems to have been a pioneer. There was a rectilinear extension north-east of the town ditch. It comprised St James, Middle and Canon Streets. It was probably linked to the relocation of the priory away from the castle in 1158. Presumably it was a piece of estate development by the canons to enhance their income (Bush and Aston 1984 77). Encroachment on to the street also seems to have begun early there. The first permission to roof a stall was given *c.*1266 for a payment of 4d (Bush 1975 56). This was presumably a transformation from a market-day bench to what in Somerset was called a shammells or shambles and comprised a permanently fixed and roofed bench (such as still survives in Shepton Mallet, *15*). Conversion to a two-room unit of shop with solar over presumably came later. The High Cross was also in place there by 1320/1 (Bush and Aston 1984 77). At Wells later growth phases can be dated. Tor Street was laid out in the first half of the thirteenth century. It was connected with the diversion of the Shepton Mallet road to enlarge the bishop's park. The single straight back boundary shows a uniform creation. Tucker Street was even later dating from the late thirteenth and early fourteenth centuries. This was a matter of individual owners and occupiers dividing plots for housing and tentering racks. Both surviving documents and the variation in plot size and depth demonstrate the individualistic nature of development here (Scrase 1989a 55 & 76-8; Scrase and Hasler 2002 20-1).

Individual buildings can be informative. Parish churches are an obvious starting point as they endure. Major phases of refurbishment or rebuilding indicate likely periods of prosperity. Extensions such as additional aisles may indicate town growth. The survival of other buildings is more patchy, but high-class buildings from any period indicate the presence of wealthy citizens. Conversely, a high degree of survival from an early period may indicate that the town subsequently languished. A good example is Axbridge where High Street has a large number of timber frames although some are disguised behind plaster. The lack of Georgian rebuilding on a major road suggests that the eighteenth century was not a good time for the town.

Having reviewed our sources we can now turn to what they tell us about the fortunes of the towns of Somerset.

CHAPTER 2

THE FOURTEENTH CENTURY

THE FAILED TOWNS

It is useful to begin with the places that are not covered in the tables. Downend, Rackley, Merefield and Southwick do not appear. Newport is recorded only in 1334 when it paid a mere 8s 4d. This sum was so low that only 49 (non-urban) places in the county paid less and several of these were subdivisions of more usual units for example parts of Wedmore and Obridge (Glasscock 1975 262-3 & 265). It seems safe to assume that all these five efforts of town foundation had proved abortive or that the places had lost any urban characteristics they might have possessed by the second quarter of the fourteenth century. However, it should be noted that Rackley had more success as a port as there was a dispute in 1390 that mentions cargoes of salt, iron and fish (Bettey 1986 59).

THE 1327 LAY SUBSIDY

Turning to the 1327 returns it is useful to begin by considering the nature of the payers. They were an affluent minority. Wells had 64 payers. Later in the century the town's population was just over 1,800. By that time it had certainly dwindled as less accessible plots, for example at the north end of New Street or along the long cul-de-sac of Moniers Lane, had been abandoned (Scrase 1989a 67 and 1989b 134-7). So it is not unreasonable to postulate a population of about 2,000 in 1327, in which case taxpayers represented only 3 per cent of the inhabitants. Furthermore, this minority of payers was sharply differentiated as fig. *16* shows. The top three who each paid £1 contributed nearly 30 per cent of the town's payment while the top seven paid just under half (48.8 per cent) and the top 12 paid 61.3 per cent. To express this in a slightly different way, ⅓ of the assessed citizens controlled 78.5 per cent of the assessed wealth. In contrast, the 28 who paid 1s or the minimum 6d had only 11.2 per cent. So within the restricted

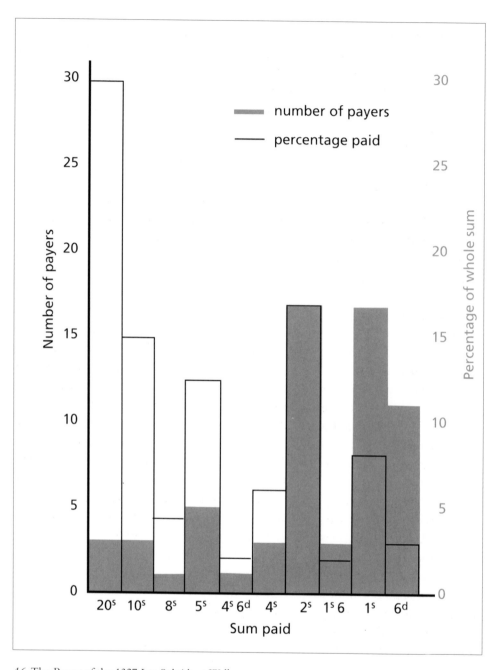

16 The Payers of the 1327 Lay Subsidy at Wells

number of payers there was a small number of a wealthy elite. Such findings are common for the Middle Ages although they relate mainly to the larger towns that have been most studied. For example Kermode points out that in 1524-5 in Coventry the top 5 per cent owned nearly 75 per cent of the taxable wealth, while the bottom 75 per cent of the population owned about 4 per cent. In poorer Yarmouth, 66 per cent were too poor to be assessed and 23 men owned half of the town's wealth (Kermode 2000 464).

This restricted elite could make a town's fortunes fluctuate rapidly. If one of a handful of the most affluent moved away for better trading opportunities or to switch to rural land-owning, became bankrupt or died without an heir willing to carry on the business, then a town's ranking could fall sharply. This was a general medieval and early modern problem. For example, in the sixteenth century the Malmesbury clothier William Stumpe filled the former abbey buildings with looms. He was noted by Leland as exceedingly rich and greatly raised the profile of the town. His son converted the business to cash and Malmesbury lost its brief national significance.

A further factor is illustrated by the returns from Crewkerne. There the largest payment was £2 (over a quarter of the whole) from Sir Hugh de Courtenay. Hugh was a feudal magnate whose family were to become earls of Devon. If he had been at another of his manors at the time of assessment the town would have been ranked some four places lower. Also his wealth does not directly reflect the town's prosperity although, like the presence of the abbey at Glastonbury or cathedral at Wells, his household must have given opportunities for trade and employment. However, this problem of resident lords should be slight in the circumstances of 1327. It was the first year of Edward III's reign. He was only 15 and real power was held by his mother, Queen Isobella, and her lover Mortimer. The subsidy was necessary to pay for Mortimer's unsuccessful campaign in Scotland. Unusually there was also a levy of scutage on all holders of knight's fees in the same year. So all who paid scutage or accompanied Mortimer to Scotland were excused the subsidy.

With these points in mind we can turn to the 1327 lists (*17* and *18*). The lists are easy to use as everywhere paid a twentieth, so the ranking by payment or wealth are the same. If this return and the others to 1641-2 are studied we have lists of just over 30 places when all are available. It is suggested that they can be divided into three parts. At the top are some nine towns that contained the most prosperous for the period. These are followed by a further 12 whose urban status was secure but were of mainly local significance. Then come a further 10 that were struggling to achieve or retain urban status or at the bottom arguably had failed.

The top group for three centuries normally included Bath, Bridgwater, Bruton, Taunton and Wells. Of these five all except Bruton was for a time the

a. Ranked by assessed population

1.Frome	67*
2. Wells	64
3. Bath	61
= Bridgwater	61
5. Bruton	60
= Shepton Mallet	60
7. Wincanton	58
8. Castle Cary	48
9. Taunton	47
10. Yeovil	43
11. Crewkerne	39
= South Petherton	39
13. Somerton	37
14. Ilchester	36
15. Ilminster	35
16. Keynsham	32
17. Axbridge	31
18. Dulverton	29
= Milborne Port	29
20. Langport	28
21. Milverton	25
22. Dunster	20
= North Petherton	20
24. Minehead	18
= Wellington	18
26. Montacute	17
27. Stogursey	15
28. Chard	11
29. Nether Stowey	9*
= Stoford	9
= Weare	9
32. Watchet	7

* some additional names
lost

b. Ranked by size of contribution

1. Bridgwater	£10-11s- 5d
2. Wells	£10- 0s- 6d
3. Bath	£8- 4s- 7d
4. Crewkerne	£7- 3s- 1d
5. Taunton	£7- 3s- 0d
6. Frome	£6-18s- 2d
7. Shepton Mallet	£6- 9s- 2d
8. Bruton	£6- 3s- 9d
9. Wincanton	£4- 9s- 4d
10. South Petherton	£3-17s- 2d
11. Axbridge	£3-15s- 4d
12. Castle Cary	£3- 6s- 0d
13. Ilminster	£2-16s- 1d
14. Yeovil	£2-15s- 9d
15. Somerton	£2-14s- 2d
16. Keynsham	£2- 4s- 8d
17. Ilchester	£2- 4s- 5d
18. Langport	£2- 2s- 0d
19. Milverton	£2- 1s- 0d
20. Montacute	£1-17s- 6d
21. Milborne Port	£1-12s- 0d
22. Dunster	£1-11s- 1d
23. Minehead	£1- 9s- 2d
24. Wellington	£1- 6s- 0d
25. Dulverton	£1- 5s- 2d
26. Stogursey	£1- 2s- 4d
27. Chard	£1- 2s- 0d
= North Petherton	£1- 2s- 0d
29. Watchet	13s- 4d
30. Weare	9s- 0d
31. Nether Stowey	6s- 8d
32. Stoford	6s- 0d

c. The distribution of wealth

Town	minimum paid	maximum paid	multipler between minimum and maximum	percentage of total wealth held by richest third
Axbridge	1s- 0d	6s-8d	6.6	53
Bath	6d	16s-0d	32.0	64
Bridgwater	10d	18s-0d	21.6	45
Bruton	6d	13s-4d	26.6	70
Castle Cary	6d	£1-0s-0d	40.0	64
Chard	7d	3s-0d	10.3	50
Crewkerne	10d	£2-0s-0d	48.0	51
Dulverton	6d	1s-6d	3.0	58
Dunster	7d	5s-0d	8.6	56
Frome*	3d	5s-2d	21.0	49
Ilchester	6d	2s-6d	5.0	47
Ilminster	9d	5s-9d	7.6	68
Keynsham	6d	4s-0d	8.0	58
Langport	6d	6s-0d	6.0	58
Milborne Port	6d	2s-0d	4.0	48
Milverton	7d	5s-0d	8.7	57
Minehead	7d	10s-0d	17.1	68
Montacute	6d	6s-0d	12.0	56
Nether Stowey*	6d	1s-0d	2.0	46
North Petherton	6d	3s-0d	6.0	77
Shepton Mallet	6d	8s-0d	16.0	62
Somerton	6d	3s-0d	6.0	45
South Petherton	6d	£1-0s-0d	40.0	66
Stoford	6d	1s-0d	2.0	42
Stogursey	8d	2s-9d	3.3	48
Taunton	6d	£1-0s-0d	40.0	62
Watchet	9d	3s-6d	5.3	49
Weare	6d	2s-8d	5.3	52
Wellington	9d	3s-0d	4.0	54
Wells	6d	£1-0s-0d	40.0	79
Wincanton	6d	3s-0d	8.0	44
Yeovil	6d	5s-0d	10.0	42

* based on incomplete data

17 *Above*: 1327 Lay Subsidy

18 *Opposite*: 1327 and 1334 compared by assessed wealth

a. 1327

1. Bridgwater — £211
2. Wells — £201
3. Bath — £165
4. Crewkerne — £143
5. Taunton — £143
6. Frome — £138
7. Shepton Mallet — £129
8. Bruton — £124
9. Wincanton — £89
10. South Petherton — £77
11. Axbridge — £75
12. Castle Cary — £66
13. Ilminster — £56
14. Yeovil — £56
15. Somerton — £54
16. Keynsham — £44
17. Ilchester — £44
18. Langport — £42
19. Milverton — £42
20. Montacute — £38
21. Milborne Port — £32
22. Dunster — £31
23. Minehead — £29
24. Wellington — £26
25. Dulverton — £25
26. Stogursey — £25
27. Chard — £22
= North Petherton — £22
29. Watchet — £13
30. Weare — £9
31. Nether Stowey — £7
32. Stoford — £6

b. 1334

1. Bridgwater — £260
2. Wells — £190
3. Shepton Mallet — £158
4. Crewkerne — £144
5. Castle Cary — £135
6. Bath — £133
7. Frome — £130
8. Taunton — £102
9. Bruton — £95
10. Wincanton — £90
11. South Petherton — £62
12. Somerton — £59
13. Ilminster — £54
14. Keynsham — £53
15. Yeovil — £49
16. Axbridge — £45
17. Ilchester* — £40
= Langport — £40
19. Minehead — £38
20. Milverton — £35
21. Dulverton — £32
= Montacute — £32
23. Dunster — £31
24. Milborne Port — £31
25. North Petherton — £30
26. Wellington — £22
27. Stogursey — £20
28. Weare — £14
29. Chard — £13
30. Watchet — £11
31. Stoford — £9
32. Nether Stowey — £7
33. Newport — £6

* with part of Sock Dennis

most prosperous town. All had additional advantages besides their local market functions. At varying times each had an important cloth industry – indeed, Tauntons and Bridgwaters were recognised names for types of cloth. Similarly their markets developed specialist functions. By the early modern period Taunton's cheese market was famous. In addition, Bridgwater had its harbour, Wells its cathedral and both Bath and Bruton an abbey. In 1327 the other leading towns were Crewkerne (partly due to Hugh de Courtenay), Frome, Shepton Mallet and Wincanton. So the majority of the top towns were of undoubted Anglo-Saxon origins with Bridgwater and Wells as the greatest post-Conquest successes. There is evidence to push this success back to at least the middle of the thirteenth century. For example there are records indicating the presence of a small group of Jews at Bridgwater while others visited Wells (Dunning 1992 18). They were generally drawn to the most affluent towns.

There were more foundations of the twelfth and thirteenth centuries in the middle group. But amongst them five Anglo-Saxon towns were enjoying mixed fortunes. Axbridge, Ilminster and Langport were at least holding their positions. This is most striking as an achievement in the case of Axbridge which was relatively close to Wells and had had Rackley and Lower (or Nether) Weare planted within 3 miles (5km). It must also have suffered when King John ended the royal presence at Cheddar. An occasional wealthy customer and the chance to seek royal patronage were both lost. In contrast, Ilchester and Milborne Port were slipping back. Both were in that over-dense southern cluster of towns already referred to. The decline of Ilchester is particularly striking. At Domesday it was the second town in Somerset. Dunning states that its economic prosperity was ended by the 1280s. Its mint was gone and it had lost the monastic patronage of Cerne, Glastonbury and Muchelney. Also in 1278 the courts and gaol were moved to Somerton (*VCH* iii 139 & 188).

This decline of Ilchester and Milborne Port is mirrored by their churches. Ilchester had a profusion of religious establishments at its peak. By 1280 it certainly had seven churches if St Andrew's Northover is included, together with a friary, a hospital and a lepers' hospital (Stevens Cox 1952; Aston and Leech 1977 69-70). This is a generous provision and it is significant that friars generally looked for sites in major towns. A further church, St Leonard's, which stood on the bridge is not mentioned until 1476. An almshouse was founded in 1426. By that time the leper hospital had vanished while the Holy Trinity or Whitehall Hospital became a nunnery in 1281 and this in turn had been dissolved by 1463. Only St Andrew's, St Mary Major in Ilchester proper, the almshouse and the friary were in use at the Reformation (*19*). The fabric of St Mary's and the parish church at Milbourne Port are significant. Most Somerset churches show signs of improvement or adornment in the Perpendicular style of about 1350 to

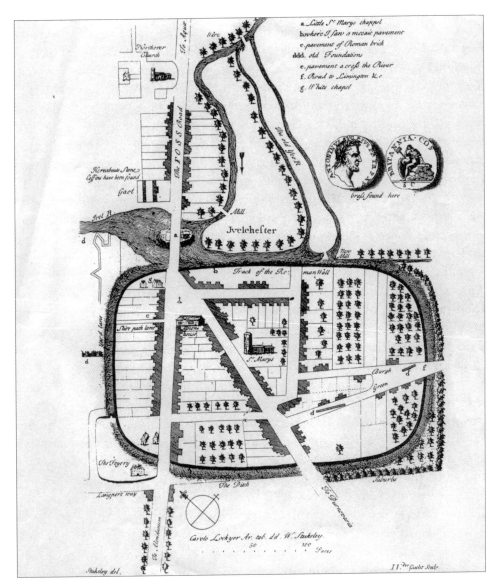

19 Ilchester. Stukeley's Map shows the town early in the eighteenth century. He provides recognisable sketches of the surviving churches of St Andrew and St Mary Major plus the sites of the chapel on the bridge, the friary and the hospital, later nunnery (his White Chapel labelled g). St Mary Minor was opposite this last while St Michael was over the South Gate. Note also how the Roman road from Dorchester here joins the Fosse Way with the market place where they converge

1540. At Ilchester the surviving church is of thirteenth-century date. At Milborne Port St John the Evangelist does have elements from the later Middle Ages but the major features are early. Pevsner described it as 'historically remarkable for its Saxo-Norman "overlap"' (Pevsner 1958b 237). Both probably reflect the closing years of the town's best period. Thereafter there were never the resources for a major rebuild to reflect newer fashions. By 1366 Ilchester was in such a state that the shire and county courts were moved back followed by the gaol. As we shall see they did little to help. Indeed, their presence seems to have done little for Somerton as it remained in the middle ranks. Its church is what Pevsner called a rarity in Somerset as it is not predominantly Perpendicular but largely of early thirteenth- or fourteenth-century date (Pevsner 1958b 289). In fact its tower, with a rectangular base rising to an octagonal top, is very reminiscent of St Mary Major at nearby Ilchester (*10* and *18*). So it is likely that Somerton did not prosper in the fifteenth and early sixteenth centuries.

Turning to the lower ranks, a number of points can be made. To begin only Watchet had possible Anglo-Saxon roots. The majority were twelfth- or thirteenth-century creations. Next it is striking that most of the towns around the fringes of the hills of western Somerset, for example Minehead, Wellington and Dulverton, fall into this group. However, the trajectory of fortunes varies sharply. Some such as Chard and Wellington were to move up the rankings. But five places, Stogursey, Nether Stowey, Watchet, Weare and Stoford, remain at the bottom of all the lists so it is pertinent to ask whether these were clear failures. The case is most convincing at Weare which does not appear after 1334 but like Newport vanishes into the larger unit from which it had been separated.

Stoford is always at the foot of these tables although it is still identified as a borough into the early modern period. However, there is other evidence. The place had a guildhall in 1361 and a separate borough court. It still had a fair in the seventeenth century (Aston and Leech 1977 126). However, that did not stop Gerard taking a jaundiced view in 1633, writing:

> now it is meane enoughe, only in greate requeste once a yeare for a plentiful fayre there kept on the feast of St Barnaby, when you may see the portgrave of the towne (for that priviledge they continew until this day) guarded with four or half a dozen copper maces walke in greate state (through the towne) though sometimes he is a man of verie meane estate. (Bates 1900 168)

So a fair does not necessarily imply urban status. Significant three-day fairs were held in a rural setting at Whitedown Hill between Chard and Crewkerne (Hulbert 1936 129-30; Bettey 1986 147). In fact Hulbert identified 94 fairs authorised by charter before 1500 and 180 days of fairs per year in 1729 (Hulbert

1936 86). All of our certain or attempted towns listed in the fourteenth century had a fair except Newport although the group that had failed before 1327 did not. This calculation includes Watchet as a place with a fair on the basis of St Decuman's Fair which was in being by 1244 and was held in the area between St Decuman's church and the prebendary house (later Parsonage Farm). This site is within half a mile (0.8km) of Watchet (*VCH* v 161). Many other fairs were at villages but some places were more ambiguous. Norton St Philip had an important fair but none of Leech, Aston, Dunning or Bettey claimed it as a town. The Centre for Urban History did include it. Also Leland passed through it twice in his visits to Somerset and on each occasion referred to it as a town, mentioning its fair on the first visit and its dependence on clothing and modest market on the second. So there is need to examine the criteria which have been employed. As stated, this is an issue returned to particularly in Chapter 5.

Nevertheless, on balance Stoford had probably ceased to function as a town by 1327 despite periodic fairs and perhaps some low-key trading. The explanation is probably due to poor site selection. South of Yeovil the flood plain of the River Yeo broadens substantially. The main river bends to the east towards Sherbourne but is here joined by the stream that today feeds the Sutton Bingham reservoir. The ford of Stoford is on this tributary. As a result the route east from the town has to cross a considerable expanse of low-lying land. Even today this area is prone to flooding especially adjacent to the Yeo. As a result the villagers of Bradford Abbas (the nearest village in Dorset) would probably have preferred to travel to Yeovil or Sherbourne although these were slightly further away as the route would have been more reliable. In fact the theoretical catchment of Stoford (see *41*) would have at times been confined to the smaller area on the Somerset side of the county boundary.

Certainly, the profile of Stoford's taxpayers is very different from Wells. Four paid the minimum 6d, four 9d and one 1s. There was no elite here and no great range of wealth. In Wells the multiplier between its minimum of 6d and the maximum paid (£1 there) is 40. In Crewkerne it was 48 over a range from 10d to £2. In Stoford it was a mere two. Nether Stowey has a profile very similar to Stoford.

Although the contrast between top and bottom is very clear it is difficult to discover much more from detailed study of the lists (see *17c*). To begin with there are obvious differences between places. In Wells the assessments are rounded off. Initially they rise in steps of 6d and then shillings. The upper sections are rounded in most places commonly in shillings but occasionally in marks so that quarter, half and whole marks (that is 3s 4d, 6s 8d and 13s 4d) all appear. But the lower parts of the list are more variable with every sum in pence between 6d and 2s appearing somewhere. Also the minimum varies. Sixpence is most common but there is a payment of 3d at Frome and sums of 7d to 1s elsewhere. Further up the lists there are some unrounded sums such as 5s 2d at Frome, 5s 9d at Ilminster and 2s 9d at Stogursey. One can only wonder if these follow from accurate declarations of goods or from a process of bargaining between assessors and the payer.

It is probably safe to conclude that the most prosperous places tended to feature somebody with wealth assessed at over 10s (so that they had a multiplier in excess of 20) and with the top third controlling over 60 per cent of the assessed wealth. We have already seen this is true of Wells, which in turn resembles the larger towns of the period nationally. Bath, Taunton and Bruton are closest to Wells although the peak of wealth is somewhat less pronounced. South Petherton and Castle Cary also seem similar but, as at Crewkerne, this is due to the presence of the lord of the manor. At South Petherton it was Ralph de Albiniaco (otherwise Daubenay) and at Castle Cary Richard de Lovell. Both paid £1 (Dickinson 1899 123 & 200; *VCH* iv 176). In contrast, Bridgwater and Crewkerne have a more even distribution. With the latter this is despite Hugh de Courtenay's payment of £2 that had to be set against 11 paying 1s and a further 11 paying 2s. The places at the bottom of the rankings lack wealthier citizens. They were presumably vulnerable as they lacked reserves of capital for either innovation or to ride out hard times. By this test Dulverton, Stogursey, Watchet, Weare and Wincanton were almost as badly placed as Stoford and Nether Stowey. Also Ilchester was hardly better situated. Moreover, Ilchester proper was very depressed as most of the better-off inhabitants lived in Northover. In Ilchester 12 persons paid below 1s and the other 11 sums ranging from 1s to 2s. In Northover payments ranged from a shilling to 2s 6d.

Nevertheless, it should not be assumed that places other than Stoford and Nether Stowey lacked urban features. They had people of modest means. Thus at Watchet there were two less payers than at Stoford but the wealth was rather greater. One paid 3s 6d, two paid 3s, one 1s 1d, two a shilling and one 9d with nobody assessed at the minimum 6d and a multiplier of 5.3 between the lowest and highest payments. Watchet is exceptional only in its small number of payers. Away from our top group a low range of wealth was common (see *17*). Furthermore, the situation in Worcestershire was broadly similar. Christopher Dyer identified some 12 enduring medieval market towns below Worcester itself (C. Dyer 2002b 4). Seven of these can be separately identified in the 1327 returns although like Somerset a number of the returns include substantial rural manors as well as the urban core. In these seven the maximum payment varied from a mere 2s at Upton to 10s at Kidderminster. The most affluent third of the payers controlled between 50 per cent of the assessed wealth at Upton and 56 per cent at Dudley. These figures are very similar to the middle range and weaker towns in

Somerset. Of the four places identified by Dyer as failing within the Middle Ages only Blockley and Clifton performed as badly as the weaker Somerset places at this time. Clifton had only 19 payers commanding a total wealth of £21 and with the most affluent inhabitant paying 3s. Blockley had 16 payers with wealth of £27 and the most affluent paying 2s 6d (Eld 1895).

Also there is more documentary and physical evidence for modest prosperity in Somerset. Stogursey generated enough demand for its market place to be colonised by small properties and for additional houses on High and Lime Streets to occupy the ends of open field strips (*VCH* vi 132-3). So it must have had a period of growth even if this had faded by the early fourteenth century. It seems likely that these encroachments were before 1307 (see *13*) as it would have been impossible for the town to have 60 burgages without them *(VCH* vi 132). Again the *Victoria County History* shows that Watchet had Flemish merchants trading there in 1210 and an expanding number of streets with appropriately urban names although it suffered storm damage in 1458 (*VCH* v 146 & 159). Even Nether Stowey had a medieval market cross and an eighteenth-century market hall although between these two phases Leland characterised it as a poor village. So perhaps it is fair to conclude that such places had at least intermittent bursts of urban activity when circumstances were favourable or somebody was willing to make an investment.

More generally it is worth noting that by the last years of the Middle Ages and probably from a good deal earlier, Somerset was well supplied with the physical equipment that contemporaries associated with urban status, that is gates (*20*), elaborate water supplies (*21* and *33*), market crosses (*9* and *22*) and a range of other crosses (*23*). The Somerset towns often outperformed larger richer places in Gloucestershire and Wiltshire (*24* and *25*). This abundance of urban symbols plus a long east–west extend probably explains why Leland described Wells as a large town which is hardly justified in terms of population.

However, the key to urban status was as much in the place's range of functions as in its wealth or townscape. Unfortunately, the returns are less helpful in this respect. It is true bynames had not yet hardened into hereditary surnames and therefore tell us something about their bearer and that the urban records for 1327 contain over 1,280 names or 12 per cent of the county's assessed population. The problem is that bynames reflecting occupation are not the most common. For example in Wells 497 names survive in all types of record for the years up to 1350 and of these 61 had some supplementary information as with Adam Loek, mason or Ralph Plomer of Wermunstre. Only 9 per cent of all this data related to occupations, whereas 34 per cent reflected the place of origin (Scrase 1989/90 26 & 33). As a result the occupational bynames given in 1327 only exceed 10 at Bath and the initial count has to be reduced to take account of duplicates and to

20 Opposite above: Langport. Few Somerset towns had gates and most were swept away by Georgian town improvements. This survived because the route over the hill was never popular with coaches or wagons and because it had a chapel on top. The only other survivor is Bath's East Gate which led only to the river bank. In contrast the gates to the cathedral precinct at Wells survived much better

21 Opposite below: Glastonbury. The town showed the attributes of a significant centre with its market cross and adjacent to it one of the town pumps as illustrated by Pooley. The pump was the westernmost of three in High Street. This cross (and presumably the pump) were removed in 1808 but the present Gothic structure was erected in 1843 illustrating a dramatic change in taste. The present cross is slightly to the west of its predecessor

22 Above: Axbridge. The market place in 1755 from a watercolour reproduced by Pooley. Note the lost market cross and butchers shambles. Towns of any pretensions had a high or market cross of this arched and roofed form. Traders paid extra for a stall under the 'eyes' of the cross. Note also the grand Perpendicular church, evidence of a prosperous fifteenth century

23 Bridgwater. A watercolour by W. W. Wheatley showing Penel Orlieu. In the foreground is St Mary's or the Pig Cross. Larger towns had minor crosses in the High Middle Ages. They served as markers on the approach to towns, as centres for the sale of individual commodities and for cults of particular saints. As a result of the last most were swept away at the Reformation and Bridgwater is unusual in preserving two. This lasted until 1830. *Courtesy Somerset Archaeological and Natural History Society*

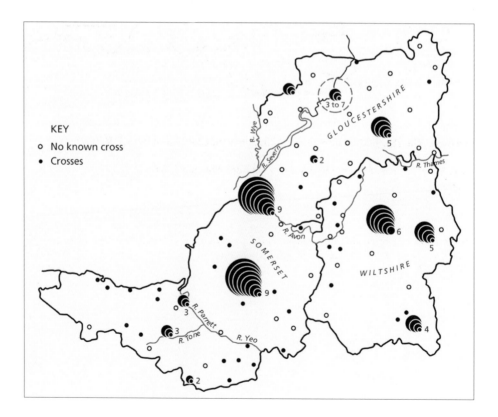

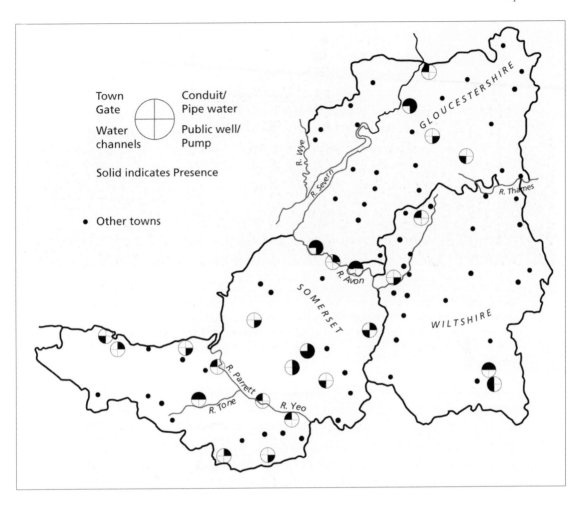

Town Gate / Water channels / Conduit/ Pipe water / Public well/ Pump

Solid indicates Presence

• Other towns

24 Opposite: The distribution of town crosses in Somerset, Gloucestershire and Wiltshire

25 Above: Other urban features in Somerset, Gloucestershire and Wiltshire

eliminate a number of non–urban types such as a swineherd, a forester, a parker and several haywards. When this is done, only nine places have five or more separate occupations appropriate for a town. They comprise our five 'best' towns; Bath, Bridgwater, Bruton, Taunton and Wells plus Castle Cary, Frome, Langport and Milborne Port. Of this second group Frome was then very prosperous and it, Langport and Milborne Port were all of Anglo-Saxon origins, suggesting that long-lasting places might accumulate trades. To support this Ilchester was next with four, while in Worcestershire, Evesham and Pershore which both had Anglo-Saxon roots similarly have above-average numbers of trade names (Eld 1895 43 & 55). Of Somerset's top group Bath had the most variety with 10 trades followed by Bruton, Frome and Wells each with eight.

At the opposite end Dulverton and Stoford had no names of this sort. They and the seven places with only one or two cannot on this evidence be differentiated from larger villages. But the material is too limited. Only a study of all available tax, property and judicial records is likely to give a full picture. At Wells such an exercise revealed some 33 different occupations.

THE 1334 LAY SUBSIDY

In 1334 the government tried a new approach. The earlier assessments had been criticised on the grounds of their inequalities and scope for corruption. Now two commissioners were appointed for each county. They were to agree a sum with the representatives of each 'vill'. The tax would be paid on that and it was a matter for the place to decide how it would be apportioned amongst its inhabitants. As a result there are generally no lists of tax payers. The commissioners were a cleric and a layman, in Somerset the abbot of Forde and John Inge.

The tax varied, being a tenth on boroughs and 'ancient demesne' and a fifteenth elsewhere. As a result payments are not immediately comparable but need to be converted into wealth. The definition of borough for this purpose was a special formulation and shows wide variability. Thus Somerset had 17 taxation boroughs (*26*) but Gloucestershire had only two, Bristol and Gloucester. Thus it excluded a place as large and wealthy as Cirencester, one as long established as Winchcombe and a number of later places with charters and burgage tenure, for example Chipping Campden, Northleach, Tetbury and Tewkesbury (although Cirencester and Winchcombe paid the tenth as ancient demesne). This technicality has led to a false distinction. If these taxation boroughs are plotted, Somerset, Devon and Cornwall look very different to Gloucestershire, Worcestershire and Warwickshire with Dorset, Wiltshire and Hampshire in an intermediate position. However, this needs to be contrasted with Christopher Dyer's careful tabulation of all small towns in the *Cambridge Urban History*. He shows that the density of small towns was high in the modern south-west region except in Cornwall which was one class lower. However, other places were as high, for example in Warwickshire, Kent and Suffolk. In fact Gloucestershire had the highest density in the south-west region with a town to every 31,000 acres, followed by Wiltshire with one to 32,000 acres, Somerset one to 33,000, Devon one to 34,000 and Dorset one to 36,000. Cornwall had a town to every 40,000 acres and Kent was most dense nationally with a town to every 22,000 acres (*CUH* i 507-9). In fact all southern England except Middlesex falls into Dyer's two highest categories. So the 1334 classifications do not demonstrate some special regional character in themselves. But, as regards Somerset, it should be noted that the scarcity of towns in the north of the county means that densities were higher than those for Gloucestershire in areas south of the Mendips.

As only seven years passed between the 1327 assessment and the 1334 negotiated quotas, we have to ask whether any changes represent real variations or merely different abilities at negotiation and exercising influence. Probably the latter is often the explanation. Thus if the regional context is studied (*26*) the position of Marshfield (Gloucestershire) is striking. It appears to be the sixth richest town in the south-west. However, it is a small place with a single wide street and a limited number of plots only founded about 1265 (Leech 1975 15-9). In 1327 it had been assessed on a mere £76 wealth. It may have been prosperous at this time due to Cotswold wool but it seems unlikely that its inhabitants could have outranked those of such larger, multi-street places as Bridgwater, Cirencester, Tewkesbury and Wells. Surely the more likely explanation is the lack of experience and connections of the townsfolk and the fact that their lord, the abbot of Keynsham, was of no great influence and may well have been more concerned to keep the assessment of Keynsham down (in which case he failed there as well).

Before looking at details it should be pointed out that the tables set out here do not accord totally with those in the *Cambridge Urban History* (*CUH* i 755-7). That is because Alan Dyer used the figures resulting from Hadwin's reworking to address inconsistencies with previous assessments (Hadwin 1983 36). These adjustments have been rejected here because the sharp changes are interesting for this enquiry. Also a number of Somerset towns, notably Shepton Mallet, Crewkerne and Castle Cary, were omitted there. Relevant tables therefore employed Glasscock's original figures.

Turning to the Somerset assessments, towns inevitably paid more as the levy was now a tenth or fifteenth rather than a twentieth. But the increase was not proportionate. In terms of the theoretical assessed wealth behind the payment most places managed to somewhat reduce their liability. Only 13 had their sum increased and of these Crewkerne and Wincanton were increased by a mere

a. Ranked by size of contribution

1. Bridgwater **T**   £26- 0s- 0d
2. Wells **T**   £19- 0s- 0d
3. Bath **T**   £13- 6s- 8d
4. Shepton Mallet   £10-11s- 4d
5. Taunton **T**   £10- 3s- 4d
6. Crewkerne   £9- 3s-10d
7. Castle Cary   £9- 0s- 0d
8. Frome   £8-13s- 3d
9. Bruton   £6- 6s- 8d
10. Wincanton   £6- 0s- 0d
11. Somerton **T**   £5-19s- 9d
12. Axbridge **T**   £4-10s- 0d
13. South Petherton   £4- 2s- 4d
14. Ilchester[1] **T**   £4- 0s- 0d
= Langport **T**   £4- 0s- 0d
16. Ilminster   £3-11s-10d
17. Keynsham   £3-10s- 4½d
18. Milverton **T**   £3-10s- 0d
19. Yeovil   £3- 5s- 0d
20. Montacute **T**   £3- 4s- 0d
21. Dunster **T**   £3- 2s- 4d
22. Milborne Port **T**   £3- 0s- 0d
23. Minehead   £2-10s- 0d
24. Dulverton   £2- 2s- 0d
25. North Petherton   £2- 0s- 0d
= Stogursey **T**   £2- 0s- 0d
27. Wellington   £1- 8s- 8d
28. Weare **T**   £1- 8s- 0d
29. Chard **T**   £1- 6s- 0d
30. Watchet **T**   £1- 2s- 4d
31. Stoford **T**   16s-10d
32. Nether Stowey **T**   13s- 4d
33. Newport   8s- 4d

[1] with part of Sock Dennis
T paid a tenth, other places paid a
fifteenth

b. Somerset in context (ranked by total assessed wealth)

Bristol [2]	£2,200
Salisbury [12]	£750
Gloucester [17]	£540
Exeter [23]	£406
Plymouth [24]	£400
Marshfield [44]	£270
Bridgwater [50]	£260
Cirencester [52]	£250
Tewkesbury [59]	£243
Ottery St Mary [79]	£200
Shaftesbury [80]	£200
Wells [86]	£190
Barnstaple [87]	£187
Painswick [88]	£186
Truro [89]	£182
Malmesbury	£115
Thornbury	£75
South Petherton	£62
Cricklade	£55
Wickwar	£53
Keynsham	£53
Axbridge	£45
Langport	£40
Watchet	£11
Old Sarum	£9
Stoford	£9
Nether Stowey	£7

Figures in square brackets national rankings.

26 1334 Lay Subsidy

pound. Two were unchanged so 18 negotiated a reduced sum. Generally the larger old-established towns were good at this with the exception of Bridgwater which was valued at £49 higher. One suspects that those liable to pay the tenth argued that much harder. Thus Wells reduced its assessment by £11. Now both Shaw's analysis of the town's cloth trade and this writer's work on rentals indicate that Wells was growing in prosperity towards a peak in the second half of the century (Shaw 1993 65-94; Scrase 1993 39-76). Certainly physical growth continued until the arrival of the plague. As mentioned, Tucker Street was being laid out in plots in the early fourteenth century and the first permanent house in the centre of High Street dates to 1345. In addition in 1343 Peter le Monier launched a major property development creating a new street, Moniers Lane. Associated with this prosperity was the presence of a series of wealthy merchants who had the ability to negotiate and use influence. In this respect the French-born Peter le Monier was probably significant. He had links to the earl of Salisbury and through him to Edward III (Scrase 1989b 132-5). In contrast little Stoford must have lacked both influential inhabitants and important friends. Its assessment was increased.

To elaborate somewhat on the growth of the cloth trade, a number of factors were involved. Partly it was technological. Fulling had traditionally been done in troughs where the power was provided by the feet of the walkers. Now it switched to fulling mills where hammers were driven by a water wheel. The streams running off the Mendip Hills were particularly suitable. The area seems to have been something of a pioneer. According to Ponting a few fulling mills were known nationally from the later twelfth century (including one in each of Gloucestershire and Wiltshire) but they were still uncommon in the region in the second half of the thirteenth century (Ponting 1957 22). In fact there were at least two in or around Wells in the first half of that century (Hunt 1893 ii 53; Kemp and Shorrocks 1974 77-8). The tidal rivers of Bristol were unsuitable and the rise of Somerset capitalists like Peter le Monier was aided by the attitude of the guilds and Corporation of Bristol. They did all they could to prevent the growth of this new industry, from 1346 forbidding the city's inhabitants to send their cloth to be fulled elsewhere. Subsequently they also banned the use of outside weavers to turn their merchants' yarn to cloth. Thus they did not compete with local entrepreneurs. After 1334 the industry at large was boosted by Edward III's policies although that was not their prime intention. He wished for Flemish support in his dynastic war with France. Periodically he applied pressure by banning wool exports to Flanders. Also one of his major sources of revenue was the tax on wool exports. This reached 33.3 per cent whereas cloth exports paid only 5 per cent. The producers of the Low Countries quickly realised that it was better to import uncoloured broadcloth for finishing rather than wool for the whole production process (Ponting 1957 23–8 & 32–5). Undyed broadcloth became a major west-country export. Early Somerset centres were Bruton, Frome, Pensford, Shepton Mallet and Wells together with the villages of Beckington, Croscombe and Rode. In contrast Bristol declined as a cloth producer.

Returning to the details of 1334, it should be noted that the reductions of wealth for Taunton and Axbridge are somewhat misleading. At the end of the roll is a separate item where feudal magnates (the bishops of Winchester and of Bath and Wells, the abbot of Glastonbury and Maurice de Berkerley) make settlements for some of their holdings. Those of the Bishop of Bath and Wells included his holdings in Axbridge while those of his colleague of Winchester comprised possessions in the hundred and borough of Taunton (Glasscock 1975 275).

What changes may have been significant? The most dramatic change concerned Castle Cary where the assessed wealth increased by £59, moving it up from twelfth place to fifth. Was this merely poor negotiating or did it also represent an improved prosperity? Many of the towns around the western hills also improved modestly which, taken with the higher national showing of Barnstaple and Ottery St Mary on the Devon side of the border, suggests a buoyant economy in that area. The most striking decline concerns Milborne Port, which had fallen into the class of marginal towns. Ilchester might well have joined it if its return had not been combined with part of Sock Dennis.

Next we can turn to the wider picture (see *26*). It is apparent that there was no fundamental geographical or economic factor that precluded larger towns in Somerset. Wiltshire and Gloucestershire each had a major centre in respectively Salisbury and Gloucester. Salisbury, in the south-east corner of Wiltshire, was remote from Bristol. Winchester and Southampton were its more immediate rivals. But Gloucester suggests a limit to Bristol's influence. It is some 32 miles (51km) from Bristol as is Cirencester, which also outranked all the Somerset towns except Bridgwater. Within Somerset Yeovil is about as far from Bristol as Gloucester while Taunton is rather farther at about 38 miles (60km). Similarly, it is striking that Devon could support not only a host of small towns but also both Exeter and Plymouth, ranked 23 and 24 respectively in the national hierarchy. So we cannot rely on a simple deterministic model to explain Somerset's lack of a large town.

Turning to detailed comparisons, it is apparent that the early Anglo-Saxon foundations in Wiltshire such as Cricklade and Malmesbury have held their positions better than such equivalents as Axbridge and Langport. Indeed only Old Sarum of the pre-Conquest towns of Wiltshire had collapsed and that was, of course, due to the shift to Salisbury. The residue in the old hill fort had the same assessed wealth as little Stoford, a mere £9. Another apt pairing is

Keynsham and Wickwar, each worth £53. Both were small and struggling in the shadow of Bristol. Their assessment also highlights the anomalous position of Marshfield already discussed.

The 1334 sum in effect became fixed and was levied whenever a tenth and fifteenth was granted. The assessment was not revised until 1524-5. Even then the new system became an additional charge. The old tenths and fifteenths continued to be voted until they were finally abandoned in 1625. So we have no more measures of urban wealth for the later fourteenth and fifteenth centuries. However, the last quarter of the fourteenth century did provide a different measure, a tax on all adults, which gives a reasonable estimate of population as against the limited numbers of persons paying previous levies.

THE 1377 POLL TAX

Figure 27 sets out what is known. The populations are slightly different to those used in the past. This is because a multiplier of two has been used rather than the formerly favoured 1.9 or earlier 1.75. This reflects recent views that the conventional multiplier may be a little low given suggestions that the house-holding poor were exempt rather than just mendicants and that there were considerable omissions in some towns (*CUH* i 536). This adjustment does not alter the rank order.

It is striking that the top-ranking towns of the south-west closely approximate to their 1334 order based on wealth in this classification by numbers of inhabitants. This is logical as richer towns will inevitably be more attractive places to settle. However, one would expect more volatility, with small places reflecting variations in the social distribution of wealth that are more apparent with lower numbers. For example one could postulate that Wells would have a relatively high population as the cathedral and its priests offered opportunities for much low wage employment. Also it had many distributions of alms at both the cathedral and parish church (Shaw 1993 230). As Wells was indeed the most populous town in Somerset in 1377 this may be true. But it is also possible that Bridgwater, the wealthiest place in 1327-34, was beginning to lose ground. Certainly there were complaints about the decline of the town's general trade (as against its port function) from the mid-century (*VCH* vi 207). As we shall see this depression was to deepen by the early sixteenth century. In contrast Wells, economy was buoyant as already explained. Besides Wells and Bridgwater only Bath and Taunton exceeded a thousand inhabitants. Together these four held just over 5 per cent of the county population.

However, the most dramatic figures are at the opposite end of the lists. Presumably small struggling towns would find it difficult to recruit migrants to

Somerset in context

Bristol [3]	12,690
Salisbury [7]	6,746
Gloucester [18]	4,478
Exeter [23]	3,332
Plymouth [26]	3,098
Wells [44]	1,802
Bridgwater [46]	1,776
Barnstaple [53]	1,576
Cirencester [56]	1,492
Bath [69]	1,140
Taunton [73]	1,078
Milverton	608
Langport	566
Dunster	326
Stogursey	260
Dulverton	232
Ilchester	228*
Somerton	216
Montacute	174
Nether Stowey	136
Watchet	136

* 128 at Northover and 100 at Ilchester proper.
Numbers in square brackets national rankings after the *Cambridge Urban History* Vol 1 758-60.

Some Somerset villages for comparison

Barrington	12
Brompton Ralph	104
Brompton Regis	260
Cricket Malherbie	30
Crowcombe	120
Curry Rivel	264
Fivehead	106
Hambridge	90
Isle Brewers	140
Winsford	192

Multiplier of 2 used to convert taxpayers to total population.

27 1377 Poll Tax

replace their losses to the plague. As a result places such as Watchet and Nether Stowey seem to have fallen below the threshold for urban functions. They fail one of the key tests of the various bundles of criteria used to define a medieval town as they lacked a concentration of population which is at least implicit in all the suggested sets (Haslam 1984 xiv-xvi; Reynolds 1992 49-50). But the most dramatic decline was at Ilchester where in 1377 there were 8 per cent more tax payers in the suburb of Northover than in the town proper. This echoes the distribution of wealth in 1327. Obviously the return of the courts had had no great regenerative effect since 1366. One can wonder how the courts and the people they attracted could have been serviced, or did many ride in daily from Yeovil, Somerton or Langport? (although Somerton seems also to have been dramatically reduced). Certainly Ilchester's 100 inhabitants must have been lost in the walled area (*19*). It is not surprising that most of the churches vanished and that the town's gates had decayed by the sixteenth century whereas elsewhere they survived to the stage coach era (Scrase 1999 31-2; Leach and Dunning 1990 20).

Interestingly, the 1379 return for Bath indicates a similar retreat to the suburbs. This is discernible as that return unlike those of 1377 lists names and streets. Therefore we know that 198 of the 328 payers lived within the walls while 112 lived in the northern suburb along modern Broad Street and Walcot Street and a further 18 lived on Southgate Street between the South Gate and the bridge over the Avon. There was a contrast with Ilchester as it had been at least in 1327. In Bath the wealthiest lived mainly within the walls. In 1379 a total of 19 paid 2s or more and 12 of these were within the walls. Furthermore, all the four richest citizens paying at least 5s dwelt in walled area (Green 1889a). However, one must treat these results with caution as the underassessment involved by 1379 could have had different impacts as between the city and its suburbs.

ALTERNATIVES TO BRISTOL FOR HIGHER-LEVEL SERVICES

This is a convenient point to return to the question of the influence of Bristol and look at the alternative locations where the traders of the Somerset towns could have sought higher-level services including more specialist goods and major port facilities.

In the period up to 1350 when bynames hardened into surnames in southern England, it is a striking feature of the locative names found at Wells that they include a group that are associated with the road first to Salisbury and then on to Southampton. Indeed one of the three most affluent citizens according to the 1327 subsidy and by far the most affluent according to the property records (*8*) was Thomas Testwode, a name that links him to the environs of Southampton

(Scrase 1989/90 29-30 & 37). These links extended beyond the thirteenth and early fourteenth centuries although we must turn to other sorts of evidence. For example, residents of Salisbury appear in Wells' property transactions (HMC *Wells* ii charters 400,406-8 & 411, 633-6).

However, the most complete picture is known for Exeter owing to its ample documentation, particularly that concerning the port which covers coastal traffic in contrast to national customs records. Thanks to Kowaleski's work with this material a comprehensive picture is possible (Kowaleski 1995; *CUH* i 467-94). Links were established early. Peter le Monier of Wells had connections there. In 1314/5 at the beginning of his career in England, he and his brother James le Petit (who was based in the family home of Amiens) established James' son Thomas as their Exeter agent.

Connections grew rapidly in the fourteenth century. In the early fourteenth century of those who imported via Exeter and then took their goods across the eastern border of Devon, 80 per cent resided in Dorset and 44 per cent of their cargoes were owned by shipmasters or mariners. By the late fourteenth century, 81 per cent of the group resided in Somerset and all but two of the cargoes were owned by merchants. In the decade 1381-91, Somerset accounted for only 4 per cent of importers and 5 per cent of cargoes at Exeter but in certain commodities they played a major role. They accounted for 10 per cent of the iron, 75 per cent of the alum, 18 per cent of the madder and 10 per cent of the woad imports. Apart from the iron, these were all supplies for the burgeoning cloth industry. Alum was the preferred mordant to fix dyes while madder was the source of red dye and woad of blue.

As might be expected, it was western Somerset and therefore towns such as Taunton and Chard which were particularly linked to Exeter, although the closest of all, Dulverton, does not feature, which must reflect its marginal position. Given Taunton's size and wealth it was, of course, its merchants who were particularly prominent. Kowaleski calculates that in 1381-91 they were responsible for 37 per cent of inland importers and 46 per cent of their cargoes. The link to the cloth trade is demonstrated by their callings. Two of the most prominent were John Cullyng and William Marchaunt who were clothiers and also exported cloth through Exeter. Another Taunton importer, John Osbarn, left a list of debtors including Alexander Waleys, one of the limited class of wealthy merchants who dominated the government of Exeter, plus residents of Barnstaple, Bow and Crediton in Devon besides Taunton, Lydiard, Ilchester and Wellington in Somerset.

The trade in alum can tell us several interesting facts about the economics of transport. It came from the Mediterranean and the Genoese merchants had a virtual monopoly of supplies coming into England. Their fleets sailed into

Southampton. So Somerset importers had then a choice of a long overland haul or a combination of coastal shipping and land transport. The choice of Exeter for the switch from coastal vessel to land for Taunton clothiers is significant. Exeter is 27 miles (43km) from Taunton. Other ports were nearer. Bridgwater is just over 11 miles (18km) away, Watchet 15 miles (24km) and Lyme in Dorset 22 miles (35km). These alternatives all had flaws. Watchet and Lyme were small and less than perfect shelter at some states of the tide and wind. Bridgwater had no problem with shelter but paid for it in difficulty of approach. Bridgwater is 6 miles (10km) from the coast in a direct line but tidal mud flats add a further 2 miles (3km) before permanent deep water is reached. Furthermore, the meanders of the lower River Parrett and the subsequent bends of the deep-water channel between the Stert and Berrow Flats doubles this distance. The difficulties of this tortuous approach were intensified by the large tidal range of the Bristol Channel. Taunton importers may have also been deterred by the extra time, risk and freightage charges involved in a voyage past Lands End and the Scillies and up the largely hostile north coast of Cornwall. As a result they selected Exeter despite the limitations of its out port of Topsham, the costs imposed at Exeter and a long land haul which included crossing the Blackdown Hills.

Some material may also have come direct over land from Southampton. Certainly by the fifteenth century when better documentation is available from Southampton, loads were going as far west as Taunton. Indeed occasional packhorse trains of woad and alum even reached Exeter. It seems likely that alum always reached the east Somerset cloth towns by land carriage from Southampton.

While Exeter's importance to west Somerset is understandable, its sphere of influence extended much further for some commodities. They could be a product with limited specialist sources, such as the church bells, which spread as far as mid Somerset. But more commonly the advantage was the amount of a commodity brought into Exeter offering choice, quality and the opportunity for bargaining. The main items in this category were wine and fish and the second will be used as an example here.

During the fourteenth century, Exeter grew as a major distribution centre for fish. The main reason was the development of the fisheries off the south coasts of Devon and Cornwall. Hake was largely caught in these waters, which also provided cod and increasing numbers of herring. In addition Exeter was convenient for imports from Brittany and the Channel Islands, which contributed more cod but also specialised in conger eels. In the period 1370-90, Kowaleski found that large numbers of fish dealers came to Exeter from Somerset and Dorset. She discovered six from each of Taunton, Langport and Crewkerne, with two from both Wells and Chard and others from Yeovil, Bruton, Wellington and Wincanton. But the Somerset contingent was not restricted to towns. Three came from each of Martock, a village with a market, and Shepton Beauchamp while Ashill provided two. Kowaleski points out that these links have archaeological confirmation. The types of fish bones found in excavations in Taunton and Langport are similar to those found in Exeter. Hake predominates and this was taken mainly off south Devon. The dealers also sold fish wholesale so that we know that Exeter fish reached Frome (Wheeler 1984 193-4; Kowaleski 1995 310-8). In contrast Bristol merchants shipped in large amounts of fish, some salted, from the ports of southern Ireland. That would have reached the dealers and consumers of mid Somerset as appreciably less fresh than fish which came from Exeter.

The catchment of Exeter is thus a range which extends to the south side of the Mendips. Furthermore, this spread is confirmed in other distributions. For example, the most north-easterly debt owed to an Exeter merchant in the period 1377-88 was at Frome. So Exeter's sphere of influence overlapped with those of Bristol and Bridgwater. This is a useful corrective to the temptation to see geographers' market catchments or county boundaries as real frontiers. In fact this is only likely to apply if they coincide with physical barriers such as major hills or wide rivers. In the south-west the interpenetrating was complete. Bristol and Bridgwater traders joined those from inland Somerset towns at Exeter while Exeter traders frequented the markets and fairs of Somerset. One of their favourites was the St Decuman's Fair by Watchet. By the fifteenth century, Bristol merchants were also both exporting and importing via Southampton (Carus-Wilson 1937 64, 70-1 & 104-5). To reverse the perspective, a fourteenth-century Wells merchant intending to import goods could have selected any of Bristol, Bridgwater, the anchorages on the various rivers of the Levels, Exeter or Southampton depending on bulk, value and urgency.

It is also import to remember that the picture changed over time. We have already seen how Exeter's links with Somerset grew in the fourteenth century. Conversely, links with Dorset ports seemed slight. This partly reflects the limitations of the county's harbours apart from Poole and Weymouth. Kowaleski reports that only one or two foreign ships stop at Lyme in a year during the fourteenth century. It may also be lack of documentation. If more was known it might well be found that south Somerset towns such as Yeovil and Ilchester had links with Bridport and Weymouth. As the fifteenth century progressed the picture certainly changed. Taunton traders made increasing use of Lyme while one prominent Wells grocer had connections with Bridport (Bush 1975 57-8; Roskell, Clark and Rawncliffe 1993 iii 19).

One last point needs to be made from Kowaleski's research. She illustrates for the south-west Christopher Dyer's point that the landed gentry were able by the later Middle Ages to cut out local towns and middlemen and go direct to more effective sources of supply. Already by the first part of the fourteenth-century custumals of the manors of Taunton and Stogumber required some customary tenants to travel to Exeter to fetch fish or salt and perhaps convey grain on the outward journey. Stogumber is over 30 miles (48km) from Exeter and within 5 miles (8km) of Watchet. Even more remarkably, the lords of Dunster and Bonvilles of Porlock occasionally sent to Exeter for fish although both places had small harbours on the Bristol Channel. One was threatened by silting the other by a shingle bar, but unencumbered Minehead lay between them. The Bristol Channel fisheries seem to have been more limited. Hancock found the main landings at Minehead to be sprats (which in the terminology of the time probably included small herring and sand eels), conger eels and occasionally the upmarket sturgeon.

Wine was also fetched over distance. The bishop of Winchester's Taunton household regularly sent to Exeter while Lady Elizabeth Bonville sent her bailiff on a four-day, 34-mile (55km) trip from Porlock across Exmoor to fetch wine from Exeter. Presumably he was buying in bulk as she spent that year at home. Next year when she spent more time away he was sent instead to buy a pipe of wine at Dunster. In contrast an agent was employed for fish purchases (Hancock 1903 235-6; Hunt 1962 32 & 66; C. Dyer 1989 309-10; *VCH* v 184; Kowaleski 1995 261, 269-70 & 285).

CONCLUSIONS

The fourteenth century is associated with disasters, first in deteriorating weather, then famine and finally plague. It might seem an obviously bad time for towns, with the situation particularly difficult in Somerset given the apparent over-provision in the buoyant twelfth and thirteenth centuries. However, Alan Dyer has demonstrated that towns did quite well in the aftermath of the Black Death. The labour shortage which followed boosted wages and this greater spending power led to demand for urban products and services. Things only began to go wrong from about 1420 when the impact of wage inflation hit the urban economies (Dyer 1991). In Somerset there was the further factor of the initial boom in local cloth production.

As a result town fortunes followed a number of contrasting paths. To begin with there were casualties. A number of over-optimistic foundations had not achieved any lasting urban status. Some do not appear in the earliest of our subsidy returns, that of 1327. Presumably they had already failed. Others were obviously in little better state. Newport and Weare make only a brief appearance in tax records. More were in difficulties having few tax payers and limited wealth, notably Stoford and Nether Stowey.

In contrast others were booming, particularly Bridgwater and Wells. Bridgwater probably peaked in the 1340s when the great Florentine merchant house and bank, the Bardi, used it as a depot to collect wool for shipment (*VCH* vi 218). Thereafter it suffered some recession more in its general trade than in its port. In contrast Wells prospered throughout the century mainly due to the cloth industry in the city and surrounding villages. Bridgwater, Wells and the other larger towns, Bath and Taunton, seem to have managed to recruit enough migrants largely to offset the losses from the plague. Smaller places were less attractive and struggled.

However, problems were not limited to recent foundations. Ilchester had begun to decline from about 1280. By 1377 its urban status was questionable. This was a remarkable transformation of what had been the county's second most significant town in 1086. Other Anglo-Saxon foundations, particularly Milborne Port, were also experiencing difficulties. This is unusual in national terms where it is agreed that the success of towns largely depended on early foundation and a site on a major transport route. The anomalous position in Somerset is particularly striking for Ilchester with its focus of main roads. Kowaleski added to these two the power and prestige of the town's lord and founder (Beresford 1967 263-70; Britnell 1981 219; Kowaleski 1995 50-1). However, Somerset lacked any dominant lay lord equivalent to the earls of Devon and it is difficult to rank the various lords in the county. Ecclesiastical lords were generally more successful but once again this does not work in Somerset where most failures were associated with the bishops of Bath and Wells for reasons already discussed. Similarly, Glastonbury could not contend with the dominance of Bristol north of Mendip to promote Wrington despite its great wealth.

CHAPTER 3

THE SIXTEENTH CENTURY

THE MISSING 150 YEARS

As explained, there was no fresh assessment after 1334. As a result there is no comparative source for the period 1378 to 1523. As the old tax system showed its faults, efforts were made to improve matters. Henry VII experimented with a land tax but that is not a good measure of urban wealth. However, the story of individual places can help to bridge the gap. Thus in 1463 Bridgwater was granted a new charter. The stated reason was the decay of the place (*VCH* vi 207). This indicates that the economic difficulties beginning to appear in the late fourteenth century had intensified and that some decline in the town's position was to be expected.

As mentioned, we get more information on transport routes in the fifteenth century due to survival of the Southampton brokerage books detailing the charges levied on goods leaving the town. They reveal a vast service area extending to Exeter on the west (and later penetrating into Cornwall), Coventry on the north and London on the east. It is thus to be expected that loads went into Somerset. Some of the county's larger towns were regular if small-scale customers. In 1439-40 a total of 1,637 cart loads and a mere 17 packhorses left Southampton for 84 towns or villages. Somerset took 30 full and one part load, just under 2 per cent of the whole, and a train of three packhorses loaded with woad. Frome took most with 14 full and the part load, while Bruton had seven loads, Wells five and Taunton four. In addition Bath was the destination of the packhorses (Bunyard 1941).

The main goods transported were the requisites of the textiles industry: alum, madder and woad. Wine was also common and there were a number of one-off items accompanying these regular commodities. They included almonds, iron, oil, soap and wax. Although Southampton carted fish elsewhere, none came into Somerset where presumably Exeter still dominated the market supplied by land.

However, the Luttrells of Dunster did have at least one load of fish shipped round from Southampton to Minehead. It seems to have come wrapped in canvas presumably as a now-forgotten aid to preservation (Hancock 1903 235).

Returning to land routes, only Frome had direct deliveries (for eight out of 15 consignments). Most of the others went initially to Salisbury where they were transferred to other carters. But two loads for Bruton went via Fordingbridge and one for each of Frome and Wells via Warminster. There were contrasts in ownership. The movement to Bruton and Wells was dominated by a single merchant of each place, Thomas Ede at Bruton and Roger Martyn at Wells. In Taunton at least three different local men brought in loads. But at Frome most was brought in by one of the major Southampton merchants, Walter Fetplace. He owned six loads of which five were routed direct to Frome. In contrast the local John Stockton owned two whole and the part load and always worked through Salisbury. This picture suggests that Frome still lacked a pronounced elite as it had done in the previous century. Presumably lesser Somerset towns had to acquire vital commodities such as alum from the merchants of the larger towns.

In 1497 Wells was fined for alleged support of Perkin Warbeck's Cornish followers. Study of the payments reveals that the distribution of wealth in the town had not changed (*28*). The sums paid ranged from £1 to £40 rather than 6d to £1 but once more a handful paid the majority. The wealthiest 13 paid 61.5 per cent of the whole and the top third 76 per cent (Scrase 2002a 44).

More generally, physical change suggests that the situation was not one of unrelieved stagnation. As the fifteenth century went on, a new mood was apparent. This is most easily seen in the rebuilding or extension of churches in the new Perpendicular style, an activity which continued well into the sixteenth century. It is worth quoting part of Pevsner's long account of Somerset churches (and particularly their towers). Here he was writing of the use of fan vaults within towers and states: 'they were hardly attempted before the last quarter of the C15: and most of them belong to the C16. They are a sign of a desire for costliness and splendour'. Most of his examples are in places discussed in this work. They are for crossing towers at Wells cathedral, Axbridge, Crewkerne and Ilminster parish churches and for western towers at Bruton, North Petherton, Mells, Chewton Mendip, Wrington and both St James and St Mary Magdalene, Taunton (*29*). It might be thought that this contradicts what has been said about North Petherton and Wrington as marginal places (and what will be said in Chapter 5 about Mells and Chewton Mendip). However, wealth could also come from agriculture – or in the case of Chewton Mendip lead – and it has already been noted that North Petherton and Wrington had large and varied parishes. Also Pevsner's other examples of fan-vaulted towers are non-urban, comprising Beckington, Ditcheat and Woodspring Priory.

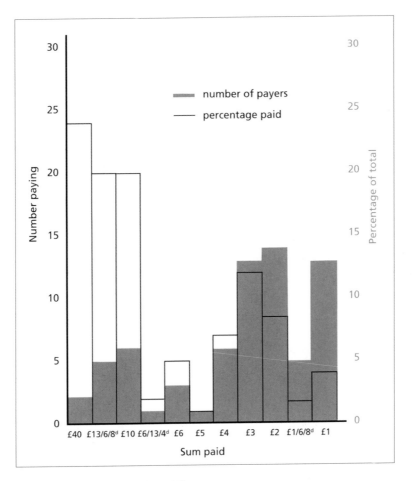

28 The payers of 1497 fines at Wells

However, this buoyant mood could spread into a phase of town improvement and beautification. This is clearly seen in the works of Bishop Bekynton at Wells. He provided a water conduit in Market Place, four grand gates around the cathedral precinct and, adjacent to one the New Works, a unified 12-property terrace. This terrace was an encroachment with the larger part built on St Andrew's churchyard but with a front strip on the highway of Market Place (Aston and Leech 1977 151; Scrase 2002b 97-8). Town councils and guilds were also caught by the trend, notably Taunton which was provided with a guild or common hall in 1467. It was built towards the western edge of the triangular market place and typically it stood on pillars to allow trading to continue below (Bush and Aston 1984 77). Some private housing also survives, notably the so-called King John's Hunting Lodge at Axbridge which is actually a grand timber-framed merchant's house of around 1500.

A VIEW OF THE TOWER OF S.^T MARY MAGDALEN'S CHURCH, TAUNTON.

This plate is inscribed, by permission, to Coplestone Warre Bampfylde, Esqr by his most obed.^t hble Servt
A. Marringall.

29 Taunton. The west tower of the church of St Mary Magdalene in 1791 (so prior to the Victorian rebuilding). It is the most splendid tower in the county and a testament to the prosperity of the town in the years around 1500. It impresses not only by height but by ornateness. Other towers have a window only at the bell-stage, not on successive floors. Again the pierced battlements and pinnacles are uniquely elaborate. However, this direct view was not available until 1780 when Hammet Street was constructed. Previously the approach from the market area was by two narrow lanes. *Courtesy Somerset Archaeological and Natural History Society*

THE 1524-5 LAY SUBSIDIES

As we have seen this was an attempt to establish a new, more broadly based system, but in Somerset we are hampered by the poor state of much of the material. Nevertheless, the returns have been studied to establish a national hierarchy and fig. *30* places the top towns of Somerset in a regional context (*CUH* i 761-7). However, it should be noted that wealth is expressed in terms of one year's maximum payment so it is not directly comparable with the total assessed wealth used in other tables. One of the reasons for this difference is the treatment of wage-earners who in many places seem to have been taxed in either 1524 or 1525 rather than both. This comment is confirmed and extended by the

Somerset material. Thus in Bath, only 139 people paid in both 1524 and 1525. A substantial proportion of the other names were indeed wage-earners. There were 47 who certainly paid in 1524 (see below) and 45 in 1525. Only nine appear in both lists as assessed wage-earners, although a further six appear in both years but paid on wages in one year and goods in the other. Many of the others who appear once were assessed on goods worth the minimum of £1. There were 56 of these in 1524 and 27 in 1525 but only 16 are named in both years. A number of the more affluent also appear only once. Sometimes the explanation is mortality. This is apparent when Thomas Chapman is succeeded by Edith Chapman, widow, and both paid £133 6s 8d. It is also the likely explanation when Robert Hochyns replaced William. The other could be death or the inevitable movement of people into and out of the town (Green 1889b 386-96).

Despite the inclusion of wages and rent, the majority of the assessed wealth in towns was in movable goods so the returns largely reflect the size and affluence of the business community (*CUH* i 765). This is certainly true at Wells where 168 of the 223 payers listed in 1524 paid on goods (that is 75 per cent of the whole). The remainder paid on wages and held just under 5 per cent of the assessed wealth (PRO E179/169/156). Four of the wage-earners are not identified by name or only by a first name. At Ilminster 95 per cent of the whole – that is 157 out of 165 – paid on goods (assuming those not mentioned as paying on wages or land did so). Five paid on land and three on wages. These eight controlled only 2.9 per cent of the wealth (PRO E179/169/180). The situation was similar at Bath. A total of 213 names are given in 1524. But it is simplest if we discount four incomplete or obscure entries. These involved one name with no further details, one person who paid on £1 but it is not stated whether this was based on goods or wages and three where the sums are omitted (two of whom paid on wages and one on goods). I have also corrected the wealth of Thomas Whelpleigh from 25s to £25. This will give a payment of 25s and then matches his entry in 1525 and gives a correct total for the parish. These adjustments leave 163 who paid on goods amounting to nearly 78 per cent of those clearly listed. There was a single payment on rents and 47 on wages (Green 1889b 386-96). Bath was very similar to Wells in that those paying on wages had only 4.5 per cent of the wealth.

Within the region the most striking change is the progress of Exeter which seemed to be emerging as a separate provincial capital for the western peninsula. There might also seem to be a more general improvement in Devon and Wiltshire but this needs to be seen in the light of Alan Dyer's comment that 'Gloucestershire and Somerset clearly escaped the searching assessment of the other counties' (*CUH* i 763). Even if that is so, it is apparent that the number of persons caught by national tax had expanded sharply, as had the assessed wealth.

Ranked by number of taxpayers		Ranked by assessed wealth (one year's maximum payment)	
1. Bristol [3]	1,166	1. Bristol [3]	£479
2. Exeter [6]	1,050	2. Exeter [6]	£441
3. Salisbury [8]	885	3. Salisbury [7]	£411
4. Gloucester [27]	466	4. Gloucester [19]	£134
5. Plymouth [44]	310	5. Taunton [40]	£86
6. Taunton [49]	300	6. Plymouth [44]	£85
7. Ottery St Mary [62]	250	7. Ottery St Mary [46]	£79
8. Cullompton [64]	245	8. Dorchester [47]	£77
9. Wells [74]	221	9. Wells [60]	£61
10. Shaftesbury [77]	213	10. Cullompton [61]	£60
11. Bath [78]	212	11. Shaftesbury [62]	£60
12. Glastonbury [80]	209	12. Cirencester [66]	£58
13. Dorchester [94]	171	13. Bruton [68]	£55
14. Ilminster [97]	165	14. Bath [78]	£45
		15. Glastonbury [85]	£42
		16. Barnstaple [89]	£38
		? Ilminster	£24

Figures on the left regional rankings. Numbers in square brackets national rankings after the *Cambridge Urban History I* pp 761-7.

30 1524-5 Lay Subsidies, Somerset towns in context

At Wells Richard Powlett and the clothier John Mawdeley each paid on £200 worth of movable goods. At Bath the three major clothiers were not quite as rich but were men of substance. Thomas Chapman and John Kent each paid on goods worth £133 6s 8d and Thomas Style on goods worth £100.

As context it should also be noted that the subsidies were taken at a time of depression. Phythian-Adams examined the economic and demographical collapse of Coventry in just this period. He attributed it to a mixture of local factors and more general problems. This latter group had three components. Firstly, 1518-9 were bad years for epidemics (Stowe's famous 'sweating sickness' and perhaps therefore influenza). Secondly, there was a sequence of bad harvests beginning in 1519 when it was said to have rained from May until Christmas. The poor yields continued for two further years and distress was widespread throughout western Europe. Thirdly, at this inappropriate time the Emperor Charles V launched an aggressive foreign policy. He soaked up large amounts of capital to prepare for war with France. Francis I's response inevitably removed even more money from trade. Demand for English cloth declined both at home and abroad. Then Henry VIII's eagerness to gain glory from foreign wars created the levies of 1522-5 which extracted unparalleled sums in taxation. This can only have made the situation worse. Indeed Phythian-Adams described the subsidies as the *coup de grace* to the weakened Coventry economy (Phythian-Adams 1979 52-63). Evidence of recession can be found in Somerset. It was in 1524-5 that the cathedral escheator's accounts show the biggest list of reductions or losses of rent while the item of former years on increases of rent vanishes (Colchester 1988 285-6 & 291-2).

Turning to the detail for Somerset, it is apparent that this attempt to enforce a new more thorough system had not ended local variations in assessment. Figure 31 illustrates the differences between the approach taken in Bath, Ilminster and Wells. In Wells the assessments on goods are once more rounded to steps of a pound or above £20 to steps of £5 or £10. The Bath and Ilminster assessors were more flexible and obviously worked in marks as well as pounds. Their two highest assessments at Bath were at 200 marks while five paid on 20 marks. Six at Ilminster paid on that sum and a further five on 10 marks. But the most striking contrast is in their treatment of those of modest means. At Wells nobody paid on less than £2 worth of goods. At Bath, 45 paid on a pound's worth and at Ilminster 27. Again, in contrast to the treatment of goods, it was at Wells that three intermediate grades were inserted between £1 and £2 in wages. So once again one must doubt the exact comparability of statistics. At Wells the poorer people at around the tax threshold seem to have been somewhat protected. Those with minimal resources in household goods, business supplies or cash escaped.

If one considers the national picture there are at least partial parallels with Wells. At York there were 874 payers and only one paid on goods worth £1. This compares with 330 (37.8 per cent) on wages and 176 (20.1 per cent) on goods worth £2. Palliser explained this in terms of the classification of those paying. York, like the other provincial capitals, had a large number of wage-earners. The 38 per cent at York needs to be set against 40 per cent at Norwich or 46 per cent

a. wealth in goods	Bath	Ilminster	Wells
£200	-	-	2
£133- 6s- 8d	2	-	-
£100	1	-	-
£50	-	1	4
£46	1	-	-
£45	-	-	1
£40	1	-	2
£30	1	-	2
£26	-	1	-
£25	2	-	1
£20	3	1	4
£18	-	1	-
£16	-	1	5
£14	1	-	-
£13- 6s- 8d	5	6	-
£13	-	-	7
£12	2	1	-
£11	1	2	1
£10	2	5	7
£9	1	-	-
£8	3	5	4
£7-13s- 4d	-	1	-
£7	-	5	1
£6-13s- 4d	3	5	-
£6-10s- 0d	1	-	-
£6	4	8	5
£5	7	9	4
£4	6	19	11
£3- 6s- 8d	2	1	-
£3	10	15	9
£2-13s- 4d	2	-	-
£2	56	42	98
£1	45	27	-
b. wealth on rents from land			
£21	1	-	-
£6	-	1	-
£5	-	1	-
£2- 6s- 8d	-	1	-
£2	-	1	-
£1	-	1	-
c. wealth in wages			
£3	1	1	-
£2	4	1	9
£1-13s- 4d	-	-	1
£1- 6s- 8d	-	-	15
£1-3s-4d	-	-	1
£1	42	1	29

31 Comparisons between the 1524 assessment in Bath, Ilminster and Wells

at Exeter. This was apparently very different from the smaller towns, he argued, citing Leicester and Nottingham. These had many assessed on goods worth £1. He thought that those with so few goods were also likely to be wage-earners and therefore might be listed in different ways. If wage-earners and those worth £1 in goods were combined, the contrast largely disappeared. Thus at York the combined group formed 38 per cent of those taxed, at Leicester 44 per cent, at Nottingham 47 per cent and at Southampton 50 per cent. He then explained York's rather lower number in terms of the lower wages in the north which meant that more escaped taxation (Palliser 1979 137). How does this compare with Somerset? To begin with, Palliser's smaller towns are more substantial than any in Somerset except that Nottingham seems broadly comparable to Taunton, but is often considered to be under-assessed (*CUH* i 762). Leicester had 427 payers, Nottingham 295 and Southampton 450. Nevertheless, Bath seems to fit his theory. There the combined wage-earners and owners of goods worth £1 come to 43 per cent of those assessed. Also, as explained, the comparison of the 1524 and 1525 assessments at Bath show some cross-over between assessment on goods and wages although not everybody in this group paid only on £1 when assessed on goods. In contrast Ilminster and Wells do not conform. The two groups at Ilminster are only 4 per cent of the whole, while Wells had nobody paying on goods worth £1 and only 25 per cent on wages. Wiveliscombe, which has not been considered in detail here, was an even more extreme case. Nobody paid on goods worth £1 while there were only eight wage-earners who all paid on £1. They represent just under 8 per cent of those assessed (Hancock 1911 257-9). Obviously other factors were at work and there is a need for more study on the smaller towns nationally.

As regards the fortunes of the various Somerset towns, the most striking change is the fall of Bridgwater from the top five. This accords well with Leland's reference to the loss of 200 tenements and what has been discovered about the sixteenth-century decline of the port. It was replaced in first place by Taunton while Wells maintained its second position. Bruton and Bath continued to perform well and the former, like Wells and Taunton, was obviously wealthy for its size. The subsidy also allows us a sight of pre-Dissolution Glastonbury without the encumbrance of the Twelve Hides. Lastly Ilminster had clearly moved forward. It was now a major cloth town.

Where detail is available, the distribution of wealth is still similar to that of the fourteenth century. This is clearly so at Wells where the top six held 40 per cent of the assessed wealth and the most affluent third of the payers controlled 84 per cent of the wealth (PRO E/169/269/156). Figure *32* illustrates this. It differs from figs *16* and *28* only in the pronounced peak at the less affluent end of the distribution. This reflects the broad base for this tax and shows a massive peak in numbers paying £2. This was the minimum sum for goods and the level of the highest wages at Wells. The 107 assessed at this sum together represented 14 per cent of assessed wealth. As we shall see, this is a foretaste of the distributions found in 1581-2 and 1641. At Bath the concentration was slightly less pronounced. The top six held 33 per cent while the top third had 74 per cent of the wealth.

At rising Ilminster, the social distribution of wealth forms a marked contrast to the last two. Ilminster had no great clothiers or merchants. The top six had only 20 per cent of the assessed wealth although the most affluent third had a more typical 72 per cent. It was a town of artisans and small-scale manufacturers but it also had one of the two best paid wage-earners in the three towns studied in detail. However, in a longer perspective the elite was not very different from the situation in 1327 when the top third had 68 per cent of the assessed wealth.

In addition, the existence at Wells of the lists of freeman elections enabled Shaw to add another dimension to the analysis. He showed the difference between the burgesses and the foreigners (in the sense of outsiders). The latter were numerically superior and contained a fair range of wealth from wage-earners,

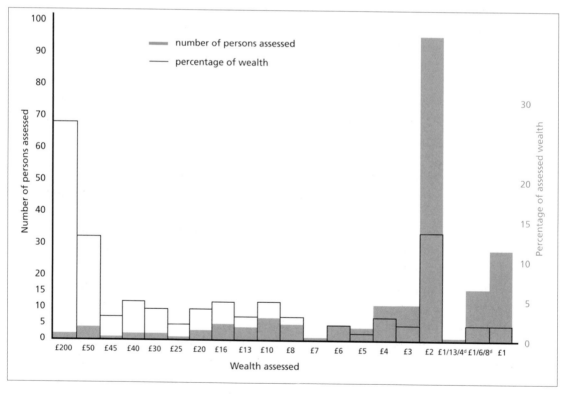

32 Assessed wealth at Wells from the 1524 Lay Subsidy

who were assessed at £2 or less, to William Vowell, gentleman, assessed at £50. But typically they were poorer. Over 80 per cent were assessed at £2 or less and their average payment was £3 4s compared with £11 6s for a burgess. Summing up he writes 'although numerically superior, the foreigners commanded only a third of the total assessed wealth in the town, and, individually, they were not even one third as prosperous' (Shaw 1993 220-7).

So the 1524-5 material seems to show us an unchanged medieval world in its broad outline despite fluctuations in the fortunes of individual places. However, dramatic changes were to follow and their impacts are clear by 1581-2.

1543, LELAND'S SOMERSET

The material later published as Leland's itineraries was being gathered for a book which was never written because of his mental deterioration. His travels in Somerset seem to have been undertaken in 1543.

His main interests were historic, so that he generally records appropriate features in towns notably castles, defences, cathedrals, abbeys, other churches, hospitals and almshouses. He was always impressed by sophisticated systems of public water supplies. In the south-west he particularly notes the systems at Bristol, Salisbury and Wells. However, he also mentions more modest arrangements such as the use of lead pipes at Bath and the channels of water at Frome (*33*). In contrast he only notes market crosses when they are of the more elaborate arched type (Scrase 2000 211-2). Despite these clear interests he usually provides a brief description of any town. These show that he had clear concepts of what constituted a town and that they could be ranked in a number of ways.

To begin, he was obviously aware that towns were dynamic and could rise or fall. Thus he commented that Poole was not an old established town but had been a poor fishing village or hamlet. Its rise was due to silting blocking the approaches to Wareham. Conversely, he distinguished between legal status in a borough constitution or the right to return MPs and an actual functioning town. The latter was closely associated with the possession of a market. Thus he remarked that Milborne Port no longer had a market but kept its borough privileges. His ranking was size-based. He identified very large towns although there were none in Somerset. Then there were large towns. In the south-west they included Wells, Gloucester, Torrington and Bridport. These were all described in some detail so it may be concluded that others treated in the same way were regarded as being in these classes. Then came places merely described as towns, so perhaps these can be regarded as average in size. They were frequently subdivided by a comment on their market which could be good or poor. Those without such qualifications were presumably of middling prosperity. Some towns

33 Frome. Any important late-medieval town featured public water supplies in one or more of pipes, conduits and canalised streams. Most have vanished but Cheap Street shows what would have been common, with an open conduit running along the street. Note also the timber-framed houses here despite Frome's reputation as a stone-built town

were identified in other ways. Somerset had several clothing towns as we shall see. Moving down in size there were little towns although there are again none in Somerset and at the bottom townlets. These were not what we might call industrial villages because elsewhere he identifies clothing villages, for example Alderley in Gloucestershire. Lastly he will often tell us if a place is 'pratty', in other words attractive.

The resulting hierarchy for Somerset has Wells at the top as a large town. It may be inferred from their detailed treatment that Bridgwater and Bath were seen as of somewhat similar status. However, he reported problems for these two in contrast to Wells. Bridgwater had (as mentioned) lost some 200 properties in recent times while Bath's cloth trade was in recession following the deaths of the three leading clothiers, Style, Kent and Chapman. His impression of Bath seems to be confirmed by the 1540 Act for re-edifying of towns. This required owners to rebuild derelict sites within three years or in default have the town corporation or, failing that, the original owner step in. Bath is the only Somerset town included although Bristol is also listed (32 Henry VIII c.18).

First amongst the middling places was Dunster with a very important market, a fair and clothmaking. Next was Yeovil with a good market. Minehead, Frome and Glastonbury seem to have had average markets while that at Norton St Philip was modest and those of Keynsham and Montacute bad (*34*). As a variation, that of Crewkerne was 'meane'. Generally, that place had little to impress him except in as much as he conceded that the market cross and town hall were attractive. In contrast Frome, Bruton and Chew Magna are listed as clothing towns although Frome's market is mentioned and presumably the existence of a market place and cross at Bruton implies a market. As already mentioned, North Petherton was an 'uplandische' or country town and the same phrase is applied to Cannington. For comparison Fairford and Northleach in Gloucestershire are similarly described (Toulmin Smith 1964 i 126). Cannington and North Petherton are

34 Montacute. A number of places which now function as car parks or village greens began life as market places. This regular square was the market place provided with the prior's extension of his town. The street name of 'The Borough' is a clue to its origins

both close to Bridgwater so this cannot imply remoteness. Perhaps they had a more rustic air than most towns. Lastly there were the townlets. We have already seen the term applied to Pensford. Mells is described in very similar terms as 'a praty townlet of clothing' as is Wickwar in southern Gloucestershire with only a variation in spelling. However, Pensford is differentiated by references to its market and fulling mills. Perhaps the status he gives to Mells, which is not generally paralleled elsewhere, could reflect Abbot Selwood's recent addition of a street. Although this was only part of an intended enlargement, it may have given the village a rather different character to its neighbours. Lastly he has quite a lot to say about the decay of the Anglo-Saxon towns of Ilchester, Langport and Milborne Port as will be seen below.

THE DOCUMENTS OF 1548, 1558 AND 1563

The very incomplete statistics available from the 1548 chantry certificates, 1558 Lay Subsidy and the 1563 Diocesan survey are set out in figs 35 and 36 respectively. They are included because they give information on places absent from other returns. Thus the 1558 Subsidy returns include Castle Cary, which is the only urban absentee from the surviving parts of the 1581-2 returns. It is shown to be a medium-rank town. The 1563 survey is significant as it gives a population for Pensford as it had a chapel of ease.

To elaborate a little on each, in 1548 returns were demanded on the goods and property of all chantries. In addition priests had to give an estimate of the number of communicants. There are four difficulties with this material. To begin with it is partial. Places without chantries did not have to respond. This excludes smaller places unless of early origins, for example Langport. In addition some priests failed to answer this question, for example the Shepton Mallet return ends with the question but the answering number is omitted (Green 1888 124). Secondly, it is only an estimate. Most responses are clearly rounded. It is also likely that accuracy was best in smaller places where the priest would have a good idea of numbers, for example the 95 at Ilchester seems reasonable while the 3,000 at Taunton may just mean a lot. Thirdly, the returns are for parishes. This would have inflated the number at Taunton as both parishes extended beyond the borough. At Wells the calculation is even more difficult as the return includes the out parish with its hamlets but excludes the cathedral liberty. Lastly there is the question of what weighting is needed to convert communicants to total population. A quarter has been added, as the age of first communion was usually before that of legal adulthood. Where that is an issue a weighting of a third is usual. Use of a quarter gives answers broadly in line with 1563 estimates. The doubtful figures are for Wells and Taunton which seem too large.

a. 1548 Chantry certificates **Towns ranked by number of** **communicants**		**b. 1563 Diocesan Survey** **Towns ranked by population**	
1. Taunton	3,000 (3,750)	1. Bridgwater	1,681
2. Wells	2,000 (2,500)	2. Glastonbury	1,540
3. Bridgwater	1,100 (1,375)	3. Crewkerne	1,262
4. Crewkerne	1,000 (1,250)	4. North Petherton	1,126
5. Chard	954 (1,192)	5. Wellington	1,045
6. Ilminster	900 (1,125)	6. Yeovil	1,015
7. Frome	840 (1,050)	7. Bruton	995
8. Yeovil	822 (1,027)	8. Milverton	903
9. North Petherton	811 (1,013)	9. Stogursey	879
10. Wellington	808 (1,010)	10. South Petherton	777
11. Glastonbury	700 (875)	11. Keynsham	646
12. Stogursey	646 (807)	12. Langport	439
13. South Petherton	506 (632)	13. Watchet	383
14. Dunster	500 (625)	14. Pensford	303
15. Milverton	490 (612)		
16. Langport	420 (525)		
17. Wincanton	280 (350)		
18. Milborne Port	220 (275)		
19. Ilchester*	95 (118)		

* without Northover

Figures in brackets population based
on 25% juveniles

35 Sixteenth-century population estimates

The 1558 Subsidy was levied on goods worth £5 or more and land yielding an income of £1 or more. Natives paid 2s 8d on the pound for goods and 4s on the pound for land. Aliens paid at a double rate or, if they were below the tax threshold, a poll tax of 8d. As a result the data is not directly comparable with 1581-2 with its different rates.

The 1563 returns (Torr 1980 86-91) were made in terms of households and these have been converted to a population estimate using a high multiplier of 5.05. This follows Palliser's claim for under-estimation (Clark, Gaskin and Wilson

A very partial survival included to give some data on Castle Cary where the 1581 records are missing.

a. Ranked by assessed population

1. Bruton	30
2. Castle Cary	29
3. Yeovil	17
4. Somerton	14
5. Frome	13
6. Wincanton	10
7. Milborne Port	8

b. Ranked by contribution

1. Bruton	£41-16s- 8d
2. Castle Cary	£21-16s- 0d
3. Frome	£14-15s- 8d
4. Milborne Port	£12-13s- 4d
5. Yeovil	£11- 4s- 4d
6. Somerton	£10-16s- 0d
7. Wincanton	£9- 8s- 0d

c. Ranked by total assessed wealth

1. Bruton	£254
2. Castle Cary	£156
3. Milborne Port	£85
4. Somerton	£75
= Yeovil	£75
6. Frome	£73
7. Wincanton	£70

36 1558 Lay Subsidy

1989 v). Generally where comparison is possible places such as Bridgwater, Crewkerne and Stogursey seem to fit relatively well with other material, notably the returns for 1548 and 1642. The sharp difference for Glastonbury reflects a single parish return in 1548 whereas both are covered in 1563.

EVIDENCE FROM TOWN FORM: A REVIVAL AFTER MID-CENTURY?

The period up to 1550 was not, of course, entirely barren. As already mentioned church improvements continued up to the Reformation, which left the new building at Bath Abbey with its nave unroofed. Also at Wells benefactions by leading churchmen, Dean Woolman and Bishop Knight, gave the town a new High Cross and a market hall in Market Place (9). Similarly Leland attributes the High Cross at Bruton to the last abbot.

Secular activity was less. In 1511 a row of shambles and shops were built over part of the market place at Crewkerne (*VCH* iv 4). That was before the hard years of 1518 to 1525. Thereafter, very little happened. The quarter-century 1525–49 was the only one in the whole period covered when there was not some major change (merger, division or redevelopment) amongst the burgage plots of Wells. However, 1548 did see the creation of a tiny plot by encroachment on the verge of Beggar Street (now the western section of Chamberlain Street) by the Priest Row intersection. This was copied and by 1584 the whole verge from Bubwith's Almshouse to Priest Row had been taken into either existing properties or used to create small new units.

It was Bath that led the way for more significant schemes. In *c.*1551 it built a new market hall in the middle of High Street. This is one reflection of a new mood of self-assertion following the suppression of the abbey. At the same time the Corporation was negotiating with the Crown about the abbey's rights in the town. These were purchased and were followed by the acquisition of the bishop's rights and a new charter from Elizabeth I.

Langport was next erecting in 1563 a thatched market house with an associated little house containing cage, pillory and accommodation for the poor man responsible for cleaning the market. In 1593 a thatched shambles was added (*VCH* iii 27). In 1571 the town authority at Wells resolved to build new shambles in High Street. In the following year they resolved to build a town hall over two of the new shambles. Shortly afterwards they built across Horse Lane. All this activity at Wells needs to be put in context. The bishop had been weakened by the Reformation and the town was deliberately challenging his prerogatives. There had been friction since 1566 and simultaneously with the building of the town hall one of the town's High Street properties was converted to a linen market. The bishop's rights over marketing and ownership of the soil were being attacked (Hembry 1967 254; Scrase 1999 53–4; Scrase and Hasler 2002 25–7 & 211–2).

In Dunster the town lord was more co-operative. In 1586 George Luttrell provided the yarn market in High Street. No doubt this helped maintain his family interest in the town. Such investment may have been desirable from two points of view. Firstly, the Luttrells had in recent years been investing mainly in the harbour at Minehead. Secondly, Dunster itself was probably loosing ground. Certainly (as we shall see), Gerard was to take a very different view of the places compared with Leland's praise some 90 years earlier.

Obviously this activity shows that town economies were improving after 1550. There was demand for both more individual accommodation and better public facilities. However, the scale of what was involved should be noted. The new premises were on sites taken from roads and market places. There was nothing

a. Ranked by number of taxpayers		b. Ranked by total assessed wealth	
1. Wells	101	1. Wells	£434
2. Taunton	81	2. Taunton	£343
3. Wellington	66	3. Wellington	£323
4. Bridgwater	58	4. Ilminster	£262
5. North Petherton	56	5. Bruton	£239
6. Bruton	54	6. Bridgwater	£235
7. Ilminster	51	7. Minehead	£227
8. Bath	50	8. Bath	£204
= Shepton Mallet	50	9. Dulverton	£191
10. Minehead	48	10. Chard	£175
11. Dulverton	44	11. North Petherton	£173
12. Glastonbury	43	= Shepton Mallet	£173
13. Crewkerne	39	13. Crewkerne	£153
14. Chard	38	14. South Petherton	£145
15. South Petherton	36	15. Glastonbury	£141
16. Frome	35	16. Frome	£125
17. Axbridge	32	17. Wincanton	£116
18. Wincanton	25	18. Axbridge	£102
19. Somerton	22	19. Somerton	£91
20. Dunster	21	20. Yeovil	£87
= Langport	21	21. Dunster	£76
= Yeovil	21	22. Langport	£73
23. Keynsham	20	23. Keynsham	£68
24. Milborne Port	14	24. Milborne Port	£58
25. Ilchester	12	25. Milverton	£50
= Stogursey	12	26. Ilchester	£46
27. Milverton	9	27. Nether Stowey	£42
= Montacute	9	28. Montacute	£37
= Nether Stowey	9	29. Stogursey	£35
30. Stoford	3	30. Watchet	£13
= Watchet	3	31. Stoford	£9

c. Ranked by size of average contribution per head on second payment of 1581 (excluding aliens paying the 4d poll tax)		d. Ranked by size of contribution adjusted to second payment of 1581	
1. Milverton	6s- 0d	1. Wells	£27-15s-4d
2. Montacute	5s-11d	2. Wellington	£17-19s- 4d
3. Shepton Mallet	5s- 7d	3. Taunton	£17-10s- 4d
4. Bruton	5s- 6d	4. Bruton	£14-19s- 1d
= Wellington	5s- 6d	5. Ilminster	£13- 0s- 4d
= Wells	5s- 6d	6. Bridgwater	£11-12s- 0d
7. Wincanton	5s- 3d	7. Minehead	£11- 2s- 0d
8. Ilminster	5s- 2d	8. Bath	£10- 17s- 8d
9. Nether Stowey	5s- 1d	9. Dulverton	£10- 10s- 3d
10. Dulverton	4s- 9d	10. Shepton Mallet	£9- 1s- 9d
= Somerton	4s- 9d	11. North Petherton	£9- 0s- 4d
12. Chard	4s- 7d	12. Chard	£8- 15s- 0d
= Minehead	4s- 7d	13. Crewkerne	£7- 15s- 4d
= Taunton	4s- 7d	14. South Petherton	£7- 5s- 8d
15. Milborne Port	4s- 6d	15. Glastonbury	£7- 4s- 0d
16. Bath	4s- 4d	16. Frome	£6- 17s- 8d
= Watchet	4s- 4d	17. Wincanton	£6- 10s- 9d
18. Bridgwater	4s- 3d	18. Axbridge	£5- 8s- 0d
= South Petherton	4s- 3d	19. Somerton	£5- 0s- 0d
= Yeovil	4s- 3d	20. Yeovil	£4- 9s- 0d
21. Crewkerne	4s- 1d	21. Dunster	£3- 17s- 0d
22. Dunster	3s- 9d	22. Keynsham	£3- 10s- 8d
23. Frome	3s- 8d	23. Langport	£3- 8s- 0d
24. Keynsham	3s- 6d	24. Milborne Port	£3- 4s- 0d
25. Ilchester	3s- 5d	25. Milverton	£2-14s- 0d
= North Petherton	3s- 5d	26. Ilchester	£2-12s- 0d
27. Axbridge	3s- 4d	27. Montacute	£2- 7s- 8d
= Glastonbury	3s- 4d	28. Nether Stowey	£2- 6s- 0d
28. Langport	3s 3d	29. Stogursey	£1-16s- 4d
29. Stoford	3s 0d	30. Watchet	13s- 0d
= Stogursey	3s 0d	31. Stoford	9s- 0d

37 1581-2 Lay Subsidy

to parallel the town extensions of the High Middle Ages. It should also be noted that much of what was built was relatively flimsy. The use of thatch is striking at Langport. At Bath the hall was replaced in 1625 and that at Wells was let with the shops beneath by 1639. So towns may have revived but they had certainly not recovered to the levels of the Middle Ages.

THE 1581-2 LAY SUBSIDY

On this occasion the thresholds were £3 for goods and £1 for land. There were two payments. On the first payment, 1s 8d on the pound was due on goods and 2s 8d on land. On the second 1s was due on goods and 1s 4d on land. Aliens again paid double or a poll tax of 4d. As a result the same wealth can lead to different total payments depending on the breakdown between goods and land. So fig. *37* is more complicated than what went before. Total wealth, number of taxpayers, breakdown between land and goods, total paid and average payment per head are all considered. The last two are expressed in terms of the second payment as more of that survives, thus reducing the need for manipulation. One point should be made about the presentation of the results. Both here and in 1641 some places include a payment in respect of corporation lands. These have been omitted for two reasons. Firstly, the aim of the tables is to rank the wealth of inhabitants, not institutions. Secondly, there is an issue of comparability. Other places, notably Wells and Bath, had much larger corporation lands which are not included.

Looking at the returns in general terms it is apparent that Henry VIII's (or perhaps more accurately Cardinal Wolsey's) effort to extend the tax base had eroded. Numbers of payers had fallen by between a half and three-quarters. Most payment was still based on goods. Only Bruton had more inhabitants assessed on land while Montacute was at parity. In contrast seven places had no payer on land. Only at Bruton and Montacute was the majority of the wealth derived from land. However, the range of wealth derived from goods is very limited, being only between £3 and £20. Only four places had a single inhabitant assessed at £20 while 16 had everybody below £10. The distribution at Wells is shown in fig. *38* and is obviously different from that shown in all of figs *16*, *28* and *32*. On this occasion the top third possessed only 41 per cent of the assessed wealth while the 61 persons assessed at £3 (the minimum sum for goods) together controlled 62 per cent of the wealth.

This in part must derive from the tactics of those assessed and the attitude of the assessors. But it also reflects a fundamental change. The towns of medieval Somerset contained important merchants. We have already seen how those of Taunton operated through Exeter. Dunning discussed John Cole, Hugh le Mareys,

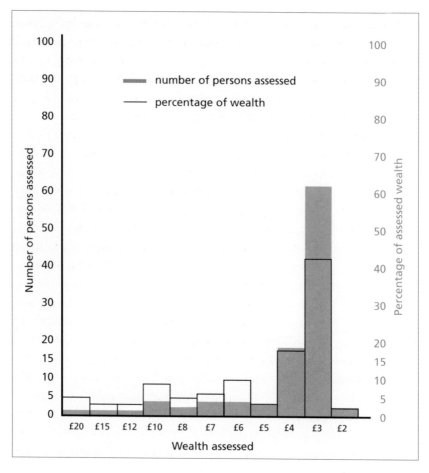

38 Assessed wealth at Wells from the 1581-2 Lay Subsidy

David le Palmer and the other fourteenth-century merchants of Bridgwater and their involvement with the Bordeaux trade together with ventures to Spain and Ireland *(VCH* vi 218; Dunning 1992 19-20 & 24-6). However, the elite are most clearly seen at Wells. One of the payers of £1 in 1327, Peter le Botoyr, was French *(CPR 1327-1330* 315) as was the leading merchant of the next generation, Peter le Monier *(CPR 1330-1334* 464, *CPR 1334-1338* 161 and *CPR 1338-40* 462). Obviously such affluent foreigners would have been drawn to Wells by excellent business opportunities. Shaw has shown that Peter le Monier was soon engaged in cloth exports while his first safe conduct mentioned wool, hides, wood and other goods *(CPR 1327-30* 16). Shaw charts the exports and imports of other Wells citizens which extended to ship owning in some cases. He mentions the *Marie* of Wells which operated out of Bristol with a Wells burgess as master

(Carus-Wilson 1937 193; Shaw 1993 89-94). He might also have mentioned Thomas Tannere, who had three ships operating either from Redcliffe in Bristol or Crabhole and Rooksbridge on the River Axe (Dunning 1983 44). Tannere also used the *Marie* and various Bristol ships (Carus-Wilson 1937 193-202).

However, such men grew fewer in numbers as the fifteenth century advanced. The Mawdeley (or Mawdley) family were the last Wells merchants of more than purely local significance. They were clothiers and two John Mawdeleys, father and son, achieved a mention by Leland who named relatively few businessmen (Chandler 1993 410). In fact the reality was rather more complicated. The freemen admissions name three successive Johns and a Richard (Shilton and Holworthy 1932 161, 166 & 171). The first John was admitted in 1492 and was one of three who paid £13 6s 8d (the second highest sum) towards the Perkin Warbeck fine. His wealth increased. In 1522-5 he was one of two most affluent inhabitants being assessed on goods worth £200. At the same time a William Mawdley paid on goods worth £10 but is not otherwise known. The second John is equally obscure. He was admitted as a freeman in 1509 but little else survives concerning him. John I died in 1540 and in his will described himself as John Mawdeley the elder. The will mentions his son John, his cousin Richard and Richard's son (another John). His assets included rural rents, suggesting that the family was beginning to distance itself from its commercial base (Weaver 1905 58-60). His son, the third John, became a freeman in 1529 and paid a fine to be free of any office, a further sign of disassociation from Wells. By mid-century the family had vanished from the various institutions' lists of urban leaseholders. Richard's house was vacant in 1550 so he had probably just died (Scrase and Hasler 2002 37 & 192). However, the third John survived until 1572. In 1559 he leased Butt Close from the town authority. This field abutted the family mansion. Then in 1569 he was listed in the Wells muster records as an esquire with a corselet, caliver and morrion (Green 1904 210). However, he seems to have played no part in the town's administration or business life but followed a career in law. By that time the bulk of family had returned to Nunney (from where the first John had come) to establish themselves as gentlemen, although it is difficult to be sure of the relationship between the genealogies given in successive heralds' visitations and the Wells material (Colby 1876 73; Weaver 1885 47 and 1905 60). Certainly a Roger Mawdelye esq. paid £20 on land at Nunney in 1558. Thereafter Wells has only traders not merchants.

At Bath there was more family continuity so the decline in assessed wealth can be detailed. In 1522 an elite of five paid the so-called 'anticipation'. We have already met three, Thomas Chapman and John Kent who paid on £133 6s 8d and Thomas Style who paid on £100. The other two, Geoffrey Francom and Henry Cavell, paid on £40 although Cavell was actually assessed on £46 in

1524. By 1540 the Kents and Francoms are missing but the other three families still provide at least part of the elite but at a much lower level of wealth. On the first payment Robert Style was mayor and he and another, Henry Cavell, paid on goods worth £40. Richard Chapman paid on £20 and John Chapman on £30. By the second collection Style had died and John Chapman had taken over as mayor. The two Chapmans and Cavell paid on the same wealth as before. Joan Style, widow, paid on goods worth £30 but she was also assessed on legacies she had in custody for John and Thomas Style worth £40 each. While some of Robert Style's debts may have been called in, the sudden appearance of an extra £70 of assets for the Style family suggests a fair measure of underassessment previously. This probably increased in 1541 when wealth apparently dropped for everyone. Cavell paid on £20, Joan Style and Richard Chapman on £15 and John Style on £10. John Chapman had disappeared from the list and instead Alice Chapman, widow, paid on only £5 worth of goods. In 1545 the assessors may have been more insistent. Cavell and Richard Chapman paid on the same sums but the others all had higher assessments. Joan Style paid on £18, John Style on £15 and Alice Chapman on £8. In addition a later Geoffrey Francom appears but paid on only £5 worth of goods. However, it is striking that during the 1540s a number of other people are beginning to match these well-established families. Two, John Sachefeld and Richard Pereman, manage in some returns to match the wealth of whoever was then the leading member of the three families but they never exceeded it. By 1581-2 the old elite had faded. John Chapman paid on £5 worth of goods. Above him there was a payment on land yielding £20, another on goods worth £10 and four on goods worth £6. William Cavell had £4 worth of goods and Matthew and William Chapman £3 each (Green 1889b 386-409: Webb 2002 179). Even allowing for underassessment, the leading families of Bath had seen their wealth dwindle and after mid-century were replaced by a new elite. However, this new elite were modestly resourced compared with the situation around 1520.

Parallels can be found elsewhere in the country. At Coventry three great merchants had paid over a quarter of the city's tax between 1522-5. The last of them, Julian Nethermill, died in 1540. He was the last of his kind. Three years earlier the mayor wrote to Thomas Cromwell about the lack of men of substance to hold high municipal office (Phythian-Adams 1979 265-6).

These changes reflect increased economic dominance by London and, in this region, Bristol. In turn this relates to greater amounts of capital needed to be able operate internationally. These costs include the increased size and sophistication of ships which greatly increased their price. More generally Everitt has remarked that the expansion of the Tudor economy led to an increase in the scale of operations. Transactions involved larger quantities and payments. This created difficulties to the rudimentary economic system (Everitt 1967 565). Also, as already explained, Bristol previously had cut itself off from the booming cloth industry beyond its limits and has issued regulations against links as late as 1479. There was a dramatic change in the sixteenth century when, for example, John Smythe was buying cloth from northern Somerset for export (Angus and Vanes 1974 4-6). Finally the Merchant Adventurers of London progressively obtained a monopoly of undyed broadcloth exports, thus squeezing the profits of provincial clothiers (Ponting 1957 35-6 & 51-2). The power of London also reduced the opportunities for the Bristol merchants. John Smyth and his contemporaries were obviously less wealthy than the famous William Canynges and his peers (Angus and Vanes 1974 3). This probably made them more willing to compete for the trade of the provincial towns around them. As a result the Somerset towns were now operating at a more modest level. At Wells the change is also shown by the contrast between four resident aliens in 1524 and none in 1581-2. It was no longer a place to attract incomers with promising opportunities.

The void left by the disappearance of a trading elite was in many places filled by a movement of the landed classes into the towns. Generally they were doing well, as agricultural prices increased in relative terms from around 1550. A number had prospered from their purchases of monastic lands. A knight now occupied the abbey site at Bruton and his contribution lifted Bruton to fourth place in terms of average size of contributions. Wellington was similarly highly placed as the Pophams had built themselves a mansion on the town's edge. Dulverton also appears to be much improved but this was due to the Sydenham presence in Sydenham House in the town centre. In fact all the other places in the upper half of the list of contributions per head had at least one gentleman or esquire except for Chard, Minehead and Montacute. But the last of these had Thomas Phellipes who paid on £20 worth of land although he is not described as a 'gentleman'. His successor Sir Edward was to start building Montacute House in 1591. Wells had no less than three esquires and 15 gentlemen. In the lower half of the list only four places had esquires or gentlemen. Amongst these Bridgwater stands out. It had a low average payment but no less than 12 persons noted as gentleman. They are obviously poorer than their equivalents elsewhere; one paid on £4 worth of goods and another on the minimum £1 worth of land. The term was obviously used in a difference sense there. Did it include retired ships' captains now living on investments?

More generally the term is used rather variably in both 1581-2 and 1641-2. It includes members of the landed classes such as the Pophams but also lawyers such as the Towses, John Baber and Alexander Jett at Wells and a number of retired traders. Nevertheless, there was a real shift in social influence and political power.

Turning to detail, the most obvious changes clearly relate to the Dissolution. All the monastic towns had suffered. Glastonbury had fallen from the top five to a place in the middle ranks. Keynsham had gone from the middle ranks to a position amongst those struggling to maintain urban status. Leland remarked that it used to be a good market town but was now poor and in ruins (Chandler 1993 429). Bath and Bruton had suffered less but each had fallen some two places in terms of assessed wealth or size of contribution. As mentioned, Bath was included in the 1540 Re-edifying Act while Leland reported a decline in its clothing industry. Taunton Priory was a smaller establishment. It is therefore difficult to attribute that town's fall to second place solely to its loss but it must have played a part. Additional reasons are not immediately apparent. Bush reports that the town's cloth trade flourished in the fifteenth and sixteenth centuries and shows how Taunton merchants contributed substantial sums towards the maintenance of the harbour at Lyme, their main port for exports. Troubles only appeared in the second decade of the seventeenth century (Bush 1975 57-8).

Detailed examination of the Bruton returns suggests that the town's position in the hierarchy was to some degree misleading and certainly precarious. By far the most affluent inhabitant was Sir Maurice Berkeley, whose mansion stood on the abbey site. In both 1558 and 1581-2 he was assessed on £100 for land. As a result he paid just over half the town's contribution in 1558 and just under half in 1581-2 (the difference reflects the extra payers caught by the lower threshold on goods in 1581-2). The next payment on land in 1581-2 was based only on £5 and the highest assessment on goods was on £7. This is somewhat surprising, as other information seems to indicate a prosperous place. Leland stated that clothmaking was a major occupation and both Dunning and Bettey cite John Yerbury who was the principle supplier of cloth to the Bristol merchant John Smythe. Also Bettey refers to a subsequent Privy Council report which indicates that by the 1630s Bruton and Wincanton were major corn markets (Angus and Vanes 1974 *passim*; Dunning 1983 40; Bettey 1986 138 & 146; PRO SP 16/187/51). Similarly Everitt's list of specialities in market towns in the sixteenth and seventeenth centuries mentions Bruton not only for corn but also malt and cloth. No Somerset town gets more mentions and only Yeovil as many (Everitt 1967 589-92). Yerbury is hard to evaluate. He does not appear in the legible part of the 1524 list and was gone by 1558. Perhaps he mainly acted as a middle man assembling cloth from Bruton and the surrounding area. In addition it is probable that a vigorous market provided much employment and benefited innkeepers but did not translate into large amounts of taxable wealth although it gave an appearance of bustle and prosperity (*39*).

This view is supported by the example of Yeovil. Its medieval rivals in Somerset had all collapsed (as will be shown below) although Sherbourne just across the

39 Bruton. High Street at about the beginning of the twentieth century. It has changed little since except for the paraphernalia necessary to deal with modern traffic. Most properties seem of eighteenth- or nineteenth-century date but a number conceal timber frames behind modernised facades. The viewpoint is close to the site of the cross. Formerly a row of butchers' stalls extended down High Street from the cross

Dorset border was thriving. Leland described the latter as in his opinion the best town in Dorset apart from Poole. Nevertheless, he mentioned Yeovil's good market and praised all of its privileges, church and chantries. Indeed the church, which is of early Perpendicular type, suggests a prosperous later Middle Ages. Also the presence of what were substantial medieval houses, but which survived into the twentieth century as respectively the Castle and George Inns (*40*), add weight to this suggestion. The sixteenth-century inhabitants seem to have had a good view of their town. Yeovil's return on chantries ends with an unrequested description that 'the towne is a great market towne and a thoroughe faire' (Green 1888 141). Nearly a century later, Gerard wrote of it as 'much increased', a situation which he attributed to the collapse of Stoford (Bates 1900 171-2). Yet it was relatively modestly placed in both 1581-2 and 1641. But it certainly had an active market trading a wide range of commodities as Everitt and Bettey have confirmed (Everitt 1967 589-91; Bettey 1986 147). This prosperity is all the more striking when it is realised that Yeovil had the most restricted theoretical market catchment in south Somerset given the proximity of Montacute, Ilchester, Sherbourne and Stoford (*41*). It also lacked the obvious route focus possessed by Ilchester. So its success must relate to other factors such as networks and entrepreneurial flair.

40 Yeovil. The George Hotel in Middle Street. This was one of two substantial medieval houses which survived into the twentieth century (the other was the Castle). Both had subsequently been converted to inns and had carried a number of names. The George lasted until 1964 when it was removed for road widening (ironically the street has since been pedestrianised). It was an example of a Wealden-style house. The previous existence of two major houses testify, like the church, to a prosperous later Middle Ages

This discussion confirms and somewhat extends the point made by Phythian-Adams some 28 years ago (Phythian-Adams 1977 36-9 and 1979 10). He wrote that, for places up to the size of larger market towns and the more modest county towns, urban quality was a function of time stating: '[it] was the extent of the rural crowds at weekly markets and seasonal fairs that transformed such places into recognisable urban centres, rather than the meagre totals of their resident populations' (Phythian-Adams 1979 10). To this we can add that this quality was also despite the slight taxable wealth of the residents. He went on to point out that the staging of ceremonies, the attraction of pilgrims' shrines or the demands of justice whether ecclesiastical or lay all underlined this transient quality of late medieval and Tudor urbanism.

Wells ranked as top town in all of total assessed wealth, number of taxpayers and size of contribution. This is surprising in that it had been experiencing difficulties in 1524-5 and was clearly in an economic crisis in mid-century. This was related to both problems in the cloth trade and the impact of the Reformation. The Hospital of St John and College of Montroy had both been dissolved. Also (and probably more seriously) the bishops had lost many of their manors to both monarchs and courtiers so the importance of the bishops in national terms fell sharply (Hembry 1967 5-40 & 254). The loss of money and visitors to the town meant that both the major landlords (the town authority and the dean and chapter) had been forced to make substantial cuts in their rents. The yield of the town authority's urban properties fell by 15.5 per cent. The early development of charities provides further evidence of widespread distress. In 1554 Richard Bramston *alias* Smith bequeathed £100 for a rotating fund for 10 youngsters (Weaver 1905 154). Subsequently in 1558 Walter Cretinge, archdeacon of Bath and overseer of Bramston's will, left £60 for a revolving fund to aid poor burgesses (HMC *Wells* ii charter 786 707). This second was two years before a similar scheme at York that Palliser regarded as early of its kind and a significant index of economic distress (Palliser 1979 86). The town authority's rentals had recovered by 1584. Nevertheless, it seems likely that Wells' emergence as top town meant that it had suffered less than its rivals, not that its economy was buoyant.

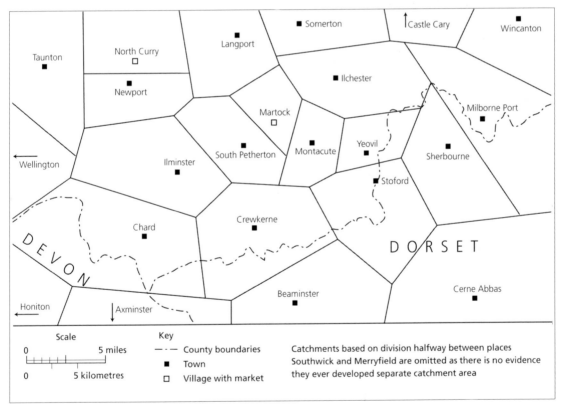

41 Theoretical market catchments for towns and service villages in South Somerset and adjacent parts of Devon and Somerset

42 Stogursey. The
junction of High Street
and St Andrew Street, with
the stump of the market
cross at the head of the
latter. Obviously Stogursey
could not afford to rebuild
in the popular arched style
after about 1350. It is a
testament to the lightness
of traffic that it has
survived *in situ*. A similar
but larger fragment at
Milbourne Port was sited
on a main road and was
relocated to a green verge
near the church

The other four towns in the top ranks are a mixed batch. Ilminster was continuing to enjoy the prosperity apparent in 1524-5 but its position was boosted by the presence of Henry Wallrond esq., George Sydenham gent, and Nicholas Balche, gent who were assessed respectively at £20, £8 and £3 on land. None of these three families was represented in the town in 1524. Wellington was similarly effected by the inclusion of John Popham esq. assessed at £50 on land while Dulverton had Henry Sydenham esq. who paid on land worth £40. However, it should be noted that the absence of this array of gentry would only have depressed any of the towns by some two places in the ranking. The other town to have progressed was Minehead. Here the wealth was mainly generated by goods with only three persons paying the minimum £1 on land. The reason was its emergence as the main port on the west Somerset coast replacing storm-damaged Watchet, silted Dunster and Porlock. It was important for a short sea-crossing to Ireland and Leland reported it full of Irishmen. This new importance was reflected in Elizabeth I's grant of the town's first charter.

Within the middle ranks the most spectacular improvement was by Chard. This had ranked 26 on assessed wealth in 1327 and had fallen to 29 in 1334. Now it was tenth. Besides the usual Stoford, Nether Stowey, Stogursey (*42*) and Watchet, all of Yeovil's rivals in southern Somerset had now joined the strugglers. This confirms Leland's unfavourable impressions of them. Ilchester he described as having fallen into spectacular decay so as to suggest the devastation inflicted by an army. He says that there were four churches within living memory but only one was still used. Another had vanished and two were in ruins. He seems to regard Milborne Port as a failed town contrasting the lost market with preserved privileges. Montacute was a poor market. The subsidy returns seem to suggest that it had lost most urban functions except on market day. Most of its wealth came from land. This decline helps to explain why Sir Edward Phellips was able to remove much of the second phase of town development to build his mansion (Aston and Leech 105-6). Similarly Langport was said to be now in decline.

So the sixteenth century was not a good time generally for Somerset towns. While there were individual success stories, most experienced checks and dislocation. When town development picked up after 1550 the scale was very different to that of the Middle Ages. Wells emerged as top town not by innovation but by showing more resilience than its rivals. Also more towns were falling under the dominance of landed gentry and lawyers. These groups were interested in power and influence rather than economic success. Indeed, new enterprise might be regarded as undesirable if it threatened influence.

CHAPTER 4

THE SEVENTEENTH CENTURY AND AFTER

1633, GERARD'S SOMERSET

As Bates has shown, the manuscript written by Thomas Gerard was part of a wave of antiquarian-orientated literature that appeared in the wake of Camden's *Britannia*. It was intended for publication and more of the county was covered than the section which survived (Bates 1900 xvii-xxi). Gerard's main interests seem to have been antiquities and particularly the descent and arms of the landed families in the places he described. Nevertheless, like Leland he obviously had a mental model of what made a town and how they might be graded. Again he could distinguish between an urban constitution and a functioning town as his comments on Stoford (already quoted) show.

Taunton was (he wrote) the most impressive of the places described. It was a fair and pleasant town that equalled or surpassed any in the county. He adds that this was despite diverse other little market towns around it. This is surprising as Bush has discovered records that the cloth industry was in decay by 1617 and as a result the town was 'greatly impoverished' by 1622 (Bush 1975 58). This leaves a number of possibilities. The town may have recovered quickly or the previous reports may have been exaggerated with an element of special pleading. Again Gerard may have been misled by an active market, a matter already discussed. In fact the last seems most likely. The cloth industry of west Somerset was an extension of the worsted industry of Devon. By this time its popularity was fading and there was a movement to experiment with new fabrics. Besides this there was a more general recession in the cloth industry due to the disruption of exports as a result of the outbreak of the Thirty Years War. Similarly, Chard, Wellington and Bridgwater were hit (Underdown 1973 14). Gerard's surviving account does not cover the north-east of the county so we lack a view of the

43 Castle Cary. The Market Hall, this structure is of 1855 but it replaced a previous hall of 1616 which thus dates the effort to revive the market mentioned by Gerard. Pevsner suggested that the ground-floor Tuscan columns probably came from the 1616 hall. That hall would have been the final stage in the infilling of a large market place opposite the castle. The properties on its left are the results of market-place colonisation

cloth towns there. They were also in difficulty. James I's support of Cockayne's scheme to prohibit export of undyed cloths hit their industry hard in 1616. Shortly after, it too was damaged by the outbreak of the Thirty Years War.

Gerard missed the industry's problems not only at Taunton but also at Chard and Wellington because next in his hierarchy must be Wellington and Ilminster which are described as having good markets. As regards the latter he adds that it stands by clothing and the making of gloves. Next came Chard with a proper market, and perhaps Yeovil, which he thought much improved. Milverton was presumably slightly less impressive, being only an ordinary market. Crewkerne failed to impress him just as it had failed with Leland. It was a market town reasonably large but indifferently well built.

We then come on to smaller places. Dulverton, Minehead, Dunster and South Petherton were all dismissed as little market towns although he does separately refer to the port and Irish trade at Minehead. This division probably reflects the divided nature of the town with separation of the upper town around the church, the lower town with the market place and the area around the harbour. The assessment of Dunster shows a striking change from that of Leland. There are then a number of places which seem to have been rather less impressive. Castle Cary had little in it worthy of commendation but he noted that the market had been revived recently (43). Watchet had a little harbour and a small market while Wiveliscombe had a 'slender market'.

He devoted some space to the decay of Ilchester, Langport, Milborne Port and Somerton, wondering at Ilchester that there was so little remnant of so great a place. He stated that Somerton was kept going by its market and fairs. He also reports the continuation of weekly markets at Ilchester and Langport. In contrast he reports the loss of the market at Milborne Port but he still termed it a town although a straggling one. This either implies he had a rather different idea of what made a town to Leland or he had noted the first signs of revival which the *Victoria County History* dates to about this time (*VCH* vii 147). The only other place he describes as a town without reference to a market is Porlock. It was another place he could not commend. Lastly, at the bottom of his implied hierarchy came Stoford, which to him was obviously no longer a town and the pretensions of its portreeve ridiculous.

SHIP MONEY 1634-9

Neither the National Archives or the Somerset Record Office preserve any of the assessments for Ship Money. However, a little does survive as some of the writs were copied into the Wells Convocation Act Book. As a result we know that only nine places were regarded as 'boroughs, cities and towns' and assessed separately in the writ. They were Taunton assessed at £100, Bath and Bridgwater assessed at £70 each, Wells and Minehead at £60 each, Ilchester, Axbridge and Yeovil at £30 each and Langport at £20. Other towns had to contribute to their hundred's share of the levy of £7,520 on the rest of the county (Nott and Hasler 2004 679 & 780). Obviously this is fewer recognised towns than in 1334 and the nine are an interesting mix. We have the four leading towns of Bath, Bridgwater, Taunton and Wells (and perhaps a tacit recognition of the decline of Bruton). There are also the three Anglo-Saxon foundations of Ilchester, Axbridge and Langport which feature despite their decline in wealth and importance. In contrast Minehead is recognised as now a place of significance. Yeovil's inclusion seems to confirm what was said in the previous chapter about its importance as a market centre.

The Wells records also include the list of 1637 payments made in the cathedral liberty (*ibid* 706-7). These were of interest to the corporation as they engaged in a long and successful dispute with Wells Forum Hundred as to whether the £12 due from the liberty should form part of the £60 due from the city or the £190 due from the rest of the hundred. As it was added to the town's contribution the townsfolk only had to find £48. The list is also of interest as clergy also paid. In fact the bishop, dean and canons paid over twice as much as the lay population of the Liberty. Even so, the weighting between borough and Liberty meant that the laity of the Liberty contributed over 8 per cent of all the laity's payment, compared with 6 per cent in 1581–2.

In contrast, comparisons with other assessments, particularly in the following decade, show that Taunton was over-assessed and that the inhabitants of Axbridge, Ilchester and Langport paid for their towns' former prominence.

THE DOCUMENTS OF 1641–2

These were the years of crisis that culminated in the Civil War. The English Army had already been defeated by the Scottish Covenanters. This created an urgent need for money to pay off the troops. The subsequent Catholic rising in Ireland produced more financial demands and also requirements that adult males affirmed their loyalty. In December 1640 Parliament voted emergency financial aid which was approved by the King in February 1641. It provided for four entire subsidies to be taken in two separate parts, the first by 27 February and the second by 15 April. The payment was to be 8s on land worth £1 and 4s for each £1 worth of goods which meant a minimum payment on goods of 12s as the threshold there was £3. The measure was for the relief of His Majesty's army and the northern part of the kingdom. A subsequent act provided for two more subsidies to be paid by 20 November. Then in July 'an act for the speedie provision of money for disbanding the armies and settling the peace of the two Kingdoms of England and Scotland' was passed. This provided for a graduated poll tax. Payment was made in three different ways. Firstly, it was done by rank where appropriate. Nobles, gentry, office holders under the crown, clergy, lawyers, aldermen, livery men and merchants had to pay prescribed sums ranging from £100 for a duke, through £60 for a bishop and £10 for an esquire down to £3 for an attorney. Secondly, there was a tax on income from all sources for anybody below the listed grades. Everybody able 'to dispend £100' had to pay £5. From there down to £50 the payment was £2, then down to £20 it was 5s, to £10 it was 2s and down to £5 it was 1s. All other persons over 16 years of age and not in receipt of poor relief were to pay 6d (Howard and Stoate 1975 vii–viii).

In response to the news from Ireland, the members of both Houses of Parliament took an oath to support the Protestant religion, the King and Parliament. It was provided that all men should take this Protestation (or have their refusal noted) but the order was not sent out until the new year (in our terms) and it was done in the last week of February or first week of March in Somerset.

Parliament had to turn back to money raising and a new Act for 'the great affairs of the Kingdoms of England and Ireland and for the payment of debts undertaken by Parliament… and in order to surpress that most wicked

a. Ranked by number of taxpayers

1. Wells	113
2. Bath	105
3. Bridgwater	84
4. Taunton	65
5. Shepton Mallet	57
6. Ilminster	54
7. Bruton	49
8. North Petherton	47
9. Crewkerne	46
= Glastonbury	46
11. Milverton	40
= South Petherton	40
13. Frome	32
14. Chard	31
= Somerton	31
16. Ilchester	17
= Yeovil	17
18. Langport	7
19. Stoford	5

b. Ranked by total assessed wealth

1. Bath	£223
2. Bridgwater	£194
3. Wells*	£187
4. Crewkerne	£169
5. Shepton Mallet	£132
6. Ilminster	£131
7. Chard	£114
8. Glastonbury	£93
9. South Petherton	£82
10. North Petherton	£79
11. Somerton	£68
12. Ilchester	£57
13. Frome	£50
= Yeovil	£50
15. Langport	£17
16. Stoford	£7

* without the sums on nine illegible lines which were included in the count of numbers

c. Breakdown of wealth between goods and land

Town	Number of persons paying on:			Maximum assessment on:		% of wealth from land
	Goods	Land	Poll Tax (on recusants)	goods	land	
Bath	48	57	-	£10	£1	50
Bridgwater	37	47	-	£6	£4	27
Crewkerne	16	30	-	£4	£70	69
Chard	31	-	-	£10	-	0
Frome	3	29	-	£5	£3	78
Glastonbury	14	32	-	£4	£5	52
Ilchester	11	6	-	£6	£7	39
Ilminster	30	24	-	£9	£8	24
Langport	4	3*	-	£5	£3	35
North Petherton[1]	6	38	-	£6	£6	61
Shepton Mallet	20	37	-	£8	£6	42
Somerton	11	20	-	£10	£1	29
South Petherton	13	27	-	£4	£8	51
Stoford	-	5	-	-	£3	100
Wells	26	58	20	£5	£6	51
Yeovil	13	4*	-	£5	£1	8

* disregarding payment for Corporation lands
[1] three entries unclear

44 1641 Lay Subsidy

and execrable rebellion in Ireland' was passed. It broke new ground for a Parliamentary tax although it had similarities to Charles I's efforts to raise Ship Money. A fixed sum of £400,000 was to be raised and this was then allocated to counties with £16,879 as Somerset's share. Commissioners divided the sum initially to hundreds and then to parishes. Assessors were then appointed to oversee individual contributions within parishes. Parliament merely established exemption limits which were below £1 on land, £3 on goods and £10 on wages. Aliens and recusants were to pay double or a poll tax of 2s 8d if below the limits. Unlike the Lay Subsidies, persons with estates in several places paid in each. Payment was in two parts in May and November (Howard and Stoate 1975 ix-x).

As stated, these documents all survive in part only (*44-46*). For the Lay Subsidy some 16 places are available for detailed analysis. They reveal a dramatic change in the behaviour by the assessed. A substantial majority now paid on land opting at the minimum to pay 8s rather than 12s on goods. However, there was still room for local variation. In Chard everybody paid on goods as in 1581-2. But there were only three other towns where the majority paid on goods. Furthermore, the maximum payments had fallen. Nobody paid on more than £10 worth of goods and that sum was reached only in three places (Bath, Chard and Somerton). In highly placed Bridgwater nobody admitted to goods worth more than £6 while in Wells it was £5. The figures for land are distorted again by the presence of the landed classes. The maximum payment was on £70 at Crewkerne and the payer was Robert Henly esq one of the Commissioners. The return for Bruton is missing but from the poll tax it is clear that Sir Charles Berkerley would have paid a substantial sum. Away from such impacts the maximum was a mere £8 and the abiding impression of these lists is the number of people paying on the

a. Numbers paying (those paying minimum 6d in brackets)		b. Sum paid	
1. Bruton	421 (355)	1. Bruton	£87- 1s- 0d
2. Castle Cary	262 (181)	2. Castle Cary	£50- 6s- 0d
3. Wincanton	193 (161)	3. Wincanton	£40- 9s- 6d

45 1641 Poll Tax

a. Ranked by numbers paying		b. Ranked by sum paid	
1. Minehead	192	1. Wellington	£50-12s- 1½d
2. Taunton	158	2. Milverton	£38- 5s- 1d
3. Wellington	150	3. Dulverton	£31-13s- 0d
4. Milverton	125	= Taunton	£31-13s- 0d
5. Dulverton	96	5. Minehead	£26- 7s- 6d
6. Dunster	95	6. Dunster	£10-11s- 0d
7. Watchet	58	7. Nether Stowey	£3-15s- 0d
8. Nether Stowey	45	8. Watchet	£2-12s- 0d

46 The 1642 Assessment

minimum £1 worth of land. In Bath it was all 57 assessed on land and in Wells it was 37 out of 58. The Bath figure is even more striking when it is realised that a single person paid on land in 1524-5, 1545 and 1581-2 while everybody paid on goods in 1540 and two on land in 1541. Obviously taxpayers were taking more active steps to reduce their burden. The situation at Wells is shown in fig. 47. The most striking difference to earlier diagrams is in the narrow range of wealth with only six grades compared with 20 in 1524 and 11 in 1581-2. On this occasion the majority of wealth was held by those in the middle ranks paying £3 or £4. The top third controlled 54 per cent of the wealth which is rather more than in 1581-2.

The poll tax survives for only three towns but besides giving us information on those places (as they are omitted from the Subsidy material) it also reveals numbers normally outside the national tax system. At Bruton, 84 per cent paid the 6d, at Castle Cary 69 per cent and at Wincanton 83 per cent. Even so, the resulting populations, when one adds a third for juveniles, seem remarkably low. Would Wincanton only have had about 240 inhabitants, or Bruton 560? These doubts fit well with the view that there was widespread evasion. To demonstrate this Stoate quotes a note from the bottom of a roll stating 'manie of the persons rated at the 6d poll are gone awaie and are not to be found to make payment' and the subsequent Parliamentary declaration that in 'divers parts great partiality has been used in assessing the poll money' (Howard and Stoate 1975 ix).

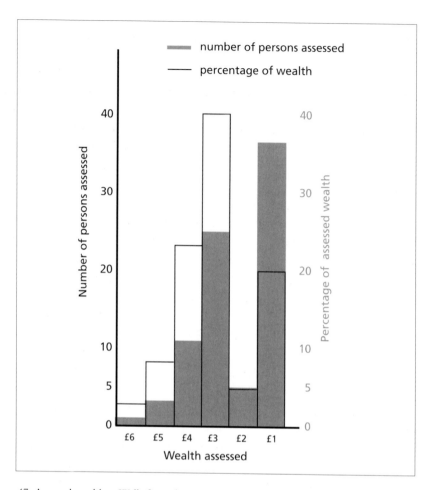

47 Assessed wealth at Wells from the 1641 Lay Subsidy

The 1642 assessment is interesting because the limits resemble those of the Lay Subsidies but far more people paid. The number of payers more than doubled at Milverton and Taunton. Surprisingly more people paid at Minehead than Taunton. Probably this does not reflect population but the lack of any elite in Minehead so that the allocated sum had to be shared round more people. Nevertheless, as explained above, Taunton was certainly suffering from problems in its cloth industry.

When all these tax records are put together with the Protestation lists (48) it seems that Wells was the most populous place in Somerset but that Bath was the wealthiest. Bridgwater had also recovered and was second in terms of wealth. Its port had revived after 1600. Joining these, Bruton and possibly Taunton in the top ranks were, Shepton Mallet and Crewkerne while Ilminster maintained its gains of the previous century. Shepton's progress seems to be linked to cloth trade despite general problems. Crewkerne's position, as in 1327-34, was in part due to a single wealthy inhabitant from the land-owning classes. At the lower end it seems likely that neither Watchet, Stoford nor Nether Stowey had the population or resources to function as towns. In contrast, Ilchester had marginally improved but Langport had further declined and its urban status must be doubted. All this fits well with Gerard's evaluation of towns except that he appears to have overestimated Taunton and Yeovil. In fact it seems that Taunton had not recovered from the depressed state of its cloth industry and was at its lowest ranking in the period covered in this work.

The gentry were again prominent in most towns and the trend was upwards. Thus Dulverton's high payment in 1642 is linked to the presence of a viscount and five esquires at the head of the list. But it is in Wells that the position had shifted most dramatically. The three esquires and 15 gentlemen of 1581-2 had given way to two esquires, 29 gentlemen and two others distinguished as 'Mr' in the 1641 Lay Subsidy returns. The 1642 Protestation showed even greater numbers although the classification is different. There was one esquire but the borough returns have no gentlemen. Instead 52 are distinguished as 'Mr' including all those classed as gentleman the previous year and still present. In the Liberty there are 14 gentlemen while the two canons present, the schoolmaster and vicars choral are designated 'Mr'. In the Liberty the number of gentlemen had risen from six in 1641.

They were a mixed lot. Some were local families of long standing, notably the Godwyns. The founder of their fortunes, John Godwyn, was a leading burgess and master seven times between 1423 and 1455. Four generations later they turned away from trade. William who died in 1557 was surveyor of Bishop Clark's lands (with the bishop's brother Thomas), served as the town's MP and married into a country family. His sons Richard, Anthony and William followed his example. William senior had acquired a rural house of some pretensions leasing Wookey Rectory from the bishop and this passed to Anthony's descendants (Hasler and Luker 1997 73-4). Richard had trained in law and served both as recorder and MP. On one occasion his fellow MP for Wells was his son James. In 1605 James was 'discommoned' as a capital burgess for recusancy following sustained absence from church. In 1610 he was reinstated and in that year purchased the Hospital estate from Sir William Dodington of Breamore (Nott and Hasler 2004 971-2 & 1026). His son, another James, appears in 1641-2 as a recusant. Others had arrived somewhat more recently but followed a rather similar strategy. John Coward, a yeoman of West Pennard, married the daughter of Thomas Leigh, a leading citizen of Wells, five times master or mayor, and who styled himself gent in his last years. Coward was of moderate means. He paid on either £4 or £10 worth

1. Wells	2,647*
2. Taunton	2,358*
3. Shepton Mallet	2,016
4. Bridgwater	1,936*
5. Glastonbury	1,389*
6. Crewkerne	1,359
7. Watchet	1,158
8. Milverton	1,092* (1242)
9. Ilminster	1,050* (1767)
10. Dulverton	969
11. Minehead	942
12. Dunster	912
13. Wellington	822* (1215)
14. South Petherton	711* (1137)
15. Nether Stowey	383

* town only, parish figure in brackets where appropriate

48 Population from the 1642 Protestation returns

of goods in 1581-2 (Webb 2002 75). However, his son Thomas was Leigh's heir and from about 1612 he was prominent in the town's business. He occupied the large house on Chamberlain Street (Reid and Scrase 1981) and married the daughter of another mayor. His son, another Thomas, married the daughter of the bishop's chancellor and initially succeeded to his father's major role in the town. He and his elder sons were all dead by 1665. The principle public role then passed to his youngest brother William who already occupied the Chamberlain Street mansion. William in contrast married into the county gentry. His wife was the sister of Sir Francis Dodington. Their son William trained in law and served as recorder and MP. He purchased the Manor of Glaston and lands at Butleigh (SRO DD/DN 92). He married first a knight's daughter and then the dowager Lady Mohun completing the family's social advance (Nott and Hasler 2004 & 959-61 & 1025).

Gentry families were also moving in from the surrounding area. William Prowse was a member of the Compton Bishop family but he took the Protestation as a resident of the Liberty and acquired an estate of local properties from the Godwyns. Wells was also a centre for recusants. Some 38 can be identified in either 1641 or 1642 compared with only 12 in 1591 (Fry 1897 115-6). In accordance with the nature of English Catholicism, a significant number of these – Canningtons, Cottingtons and Lunds – were gentlemen and they were new to the town. Other styled gentleman were lawyers – for example Tristram Towse – although (as we have seen) the law was regarded as a suitable occupation for those with landed estates or other income so the categories are not clearly separate. Some were the descendants of cathedral dignitaries, living or deceased, such as Dr William Powell's son Samuel (William had died in 1614).

Lastly, a considerable number were retired traders. The Baron family may be taken as an example of this group. They form a contrast with the families already described in that they never achieved a permanent breakthrough into law and land-owning. They were already present in the town in 1524 when two Barons each paid the subsidy on goods worth £2. John was listed under Sadler Street and William under Chamberlain Street. As is typical of this group, John never achieved the freedom. William had been admitted in 1509 but like the vast majority of those of such modest means he did not progress further and held no significant public office. By the last quarter of the century the family fortunes were improving as was shown by the careers of the brothers Thomas and Henry, both described in their mature years as linen drapers. Thomas, the elder, got a good start in that he was apprentice to one of the town elite, William Godwyn. In 1581-2 he paid the subsidy on goods worth £4. His public career was late and rapid. He became a burgess and capital burgess (in effect a councillor) in 1602, a master three months later and mayor within a year. Nott explains that this rise was due to an unexpected vacancy and the need to find somebody of means who was congenial to the dominant group. Henry, who had married the daughter of one of the elite (Alexander Towse) followed. The two were masters for a combined total of almost 60 years. The offices of mayor and JP enabled them to style themselves gentlemen in their later years. They also began to appear in the property market after 1600. In 1605 Thomas held 3 Tucker Street on an assigned lease and 31 High Street (a large prestigious property) on his own lease. Later Henry and then Henry's son succeeded him (Nott and Hasler 2004; Scrase and Hasler 2002 55, 70, 123 & 185). In 1641 Thomas' son William paid the subsidy on land worth £2 and was described as a gentleman. Henry junior paid on land worth £1 as did Helen Baron, widow (otherwise unknown but neither Thomas nor Henry senior's widow). By 1663 the main part of the family, Mrs Dorothy, Mr William and Mr James, occupied the principle buildings of the former Hospital of St John paying together over £45 rent which amounted to some two-thirds of the rents received by Lord Brooke from the Hospital site and its demesne lands (SRO DD/GS 7). By the last years of the seventeenth century, the leading family members were Charles and William. Charles was an apothecary but from 1691 he showed increased interest in property. He leased three Corporation properties comprising two cottages in Tucker and St Cuthbert Streets and a small High Street tenement. In 1696 he bought (technically as a thousand-year lease) a number of properties that had formerly belonged to a minor member of the Coward family. By 1704 he also owned a cottage and close in Tucker Street. In later acquisitions he tended to style himself gentleman as did his son, Charles junior, when he leased the Mermaid in 1723 (SRO DD/FS Box 27 and DD/CB Bundle 6; WTH 1027/7, 10 & 15). In contrast William left Wells for a time. In 1706 when he acquired a large (if old fashioned) house at the north end of New Street he is described as merchant of London. But two years later when he began to buy gardens adjoining or opposite he called himself gentleman of Wells (SRO DD/TD Box 41/3). Both male lines ended in the new century.

All this meant that Wells was changing. It was becoming a resort for the gentry or those who aspired to genteel status. Also it became a place where widows of the landed classes might spend their last days. The canonical house at 17 the Liberty was occupied by Lady Margaret Berkeley, the widow of Sir Henry Berkeley of Bruton, from 1609 to 1617 (Bailey 1982 67). In 1641 Jane Bourne, the widow of Bishop Bourne's nephew Roger, lived at 18 the Liberty and paid the subsidy on land worth £3. Unfortunately, these gentry, would-be gentry and widows did not have the resources of the main line of Pophams or Sydenhams. As a result the town was comfortably-placed as it came to rely on providing goods and services for the resident gentry. It generated considerable employment but not great wealth.

The abundant property records of Wells also enable us to investigate the degree of under-estimation of wealth in 1641. For example the younger James Godwyn paid on land worth £4. He was a recusant and therefore one would not expect the assessors to have treated him particularly kindly. As explained, he owned the estate of the dissolved Hospital of St John. Unfortunately no contemporary rentals survive but when the estate was sold in the next century it was said to be worth upwards of £68 per annum. In the intervening period Wells' rents had been remarkably stable and the estate had been eroded somewhat by occasional sales. For example in 1665 James Godwyn and Thomas White sold Humphrey Cordwent a hospital property in Tucker Street comprising a tenement and three closes of meadow (Scrase 1993 53-63 & 106-11; SRO DD/CB 2 & DD/CB Bundle 6). So it is likely that James actually had land worth over £60. Similarly Richard Stacie paid on land worth the minimum £1. He had an estate of 14 Wells properties with two in High Street, one in Sadler Street and four in New Street which were all high rent areas and the rest in the less desirable Tucker

Street and St Cuthbert Street. From the rents of adjacent properties the group must have yielded over £6 (SRO DD/FS Box 33 & DD/SAS SE24). So the under-declaration seems to have varied between six- and fifteen-fold although as Godwyn paid double as a recusant the result of the underassessment was about similar. It is as if the assessors and payer agreed an appropriate sum and then calculated the necessary wealth to justify it.

It is also possible to evaluate the apparent fall in maximum wealth between 1581-2 and 1641 by comparisons within a family. We have seen how Thomas Baron paid on goods worth £4 in 1581-2 while his son William paid on land worth only £2 in 1641. This fall is surprising. In 1581 Thomas was in the early stages of his career. Later he was to accumulate power, influence and property. Indeed there is specific evidence that his generation used their positions to their financial benefit. In 1614 a wealthy citizen, Henry Llewellyn, left £600 to establish a new almshouse. The Corporation could not implement the scheme at once as the final £100 would not become available until his mother's death. However, they could have begun to acquire land to endow the foundation or have invested the money to increase the capital. Instead it was loaned to burgesses at only 6 per cent compared with a market rate of 8 per cent. When they did begin to buy, they opted to pay in three parts. The borrowers, who included the Baron brothers and the recorder, John Baber, were so bad at repayment that the Corporation nearly defaulted. In 1632 Llewellyn's heirs took action in the Court of Chancery against this abuse (Nott and Hasler 2004 38). Both Barons were named. So one must suspect that William Baron actually commanded more wealth than his father had in 1581.

Other families indicate similar conclusions. In 1581-2 John Coward was worth at least £4 and his father-in-law Thomas Leigh £10. In 1641 John's grandson Thomas was assessed on land worth £3 while Thomas' younger brother William paid jointly with Charles Crosse on land worth £4. To put this in perspective, it should be noted that Crosse's grandfather was worth £4 in 1581-2 and since that time the Coward's had also received an inheritance from their maternal grandfather, another mayor of Wells, William Watkins. Also both had married well. Thus there is no obvious reason for a halving of wealth. Similarly in 1581-2 three members of the Godwyn family were worth £18 (of which £8 was in goods). By 1641 only one paid and that was £4 on land. Yet as we have seen they had gained the estate of the Hospital in the intervening period. Only one Wells family, the Towses, had a similar assessment in both years (on goods worth £4). Given the trend one must suspect that Tristram Trowse was actually more affluent than his uncle Alexander.

From these examples it seems that there is a sharp distinction to be made within these early modern subsidies. The fall in wealth from 1524 to 1581 seems to relate at least in part to real changes. The decline from 1581 to 1641 in contrast seems to reflect mainly an increased under-declaration of wealth. It seems that the resistance to Charles I's attempts at unparliamentary taxation had honed the nation's skills at tax avoidance. The simultaneous switch to returns in land and the evasion of the 1641 poll tax support this view. As a result the returns for the two years probably reflect relative positions within a town and are a reasonable approximation of the standing of different towns, but they cannot be used to deduce trends in town wealth over the 60 years. As a rule of thumb it is suggested that payers had increased their understatement to about half apparent wealth.

THE LATER SEVENTEENTH CENTURY

We now move on to the period without the comparative sources for the county's towns we have used previously. It was also a period when nationally urbanisation began to increase in an unparalleled way. Somerset, in common with most of the south-west, did not experience this surge of town growth. However, this lack needs to be put in perspective. As Barry pointed out, urban growth in this region did not need to be as spectacular as elsewhere as a strong infrastructure was already in place. Over a quarter of the population of the south-west already lived in towns by 1660 (*CUH* ii 67).

Only two Somerset towns were to experience the scale of growth found elsewhere. They were Frome and Bath. Change began earlier in Frome where development of the new Trinity district was underway by 1660. So when Defoe in the 1720s wrote that the town had prodigiously increased in the last 20 or 30 years he was underestimating the time scale. However, he had the correct reason. Frome was the boom town of a changing cloth industry. The industry had now switched to coloured cloths and the best products with the most lucrative export markets were now fine medley cloths. These were produced in a belt stretching from north-east Dorset through east Somerset and west Wiltshire into Gloucestershire. Defoe listed the main Somerset clothing towns as Frome, Pensford, Norton St Philip, Bruton, Shepton Mallet, Castle Cary and Wincanton.

Bath's growth started rather later mainly from the 1720s and was, of course, due to the promotion of the town into a major upper-class leisure resort centred on its springs. The 1811 census (53) shows the results of these changes. Bath, with over 31,000 people, was more than three times as large as Frome, which in turn was a third larger than Taunton, the next most populous place.

Despite losses at the bottom of the hierarchy and the movement of Bath and Frome into a class of larger towns, Somerset and its neighbours remained areas with a dense network of small towns. According to Alan Dyer, in 1673 (the year of Blome's survey) Gloucestershire had the second most dense pattern of small towns in England and Wales, Dorset the fifth and Somerset the eighth (*CUH* ii 430). He further suggests an expansion in the number of markets in the later seventeenth century although his figures for Somerset are doubtful as he is unclear on the earlier base for comparisons. He suggests a possible 31 in 1588, a definite 31 in 1673 and 35 in 1690. Barry suggested a rather higher figure for 1673. The difference arises as Dyer follows Blome, whereas Barry used a wider variety of sources searching for references to markets operating in 1673. He thus includes a number of places considered in the next chapter and perhaps better classified as villages with markets (*CUH* ii 85 & 432-5).

Dyer attributes the change in numbers to the prosperity of the rural economy (*CUH* ii 432-5). He points out that nationally the increase was due to a combination of new foundations and attempts to revive former markets. As has been mentioned, there was certainly an attempt to revive Nether Stowey in this period (*49*). He also states that the trend began prior to the Civil War in some places. This was clearly the case in Somerset. In 1633 Gerard had reported that the market at Castle Cary which had been long lost had lately been revived (*43*). Similarly, as mentioned, the *Victoria County History* dates the start of a revival in Milborne Port's fortunes to 1628. Trade there improved through the second half of the century but then fell off. A market house of *c.*1720 failed to justify its provision although it was only of modest size and had been designed in accordance with prevailing classical taste, having giant Tuscan pilasters. By *c.*1785 the arcades had been bricked up and it was later used first as a warehouse and then a school (*VCH* vii 147-9). This good period also had an impact on places which had more clearly retained their urban status. Somerton, for example, shows many signs of rebuilding in the second half of the seventeenth or the first years of the eighteenth century. This work included rebuilding the market cross in 1673.

Returning to the issue of town numbers, any other increase may be more the result of our use of the evidence rather than actual change. For the Middle Ages we rely on our judgement of places based on a number of criteria. We have seen how previous listings have varied sharply, with a reliance on burgage tenure drastically reducing the number of known towns. In contrast, in the early modern period we have a number of persons looking at places and telling us their opinion. Leland and, for Somerset, Gerard always gives us a view although their interests were mainly in other things. Subsequently, Blome, Adams and Defoe were all primarily interested in towns and their functions. Fiennes stands rather apart and her interests were more on the visual impact of places. This difference in sources may lead to the inclusion of places overlooked by those identifying medieval towns but included by early modern observers. The vital question is, then, had the place itself changed or is the difference in categorisation?

NETHER STOWEY.

49 Nether Stowey. The eighteenth-century market house from Pooley. Its provision shows that some effort was made to revive the place from when Leland characterised it as a poor village. It also shows that investment was limited

Norton St Philip is the key example. As we have seen, Leland was clear that it was a town while Defoe listed it as one of the county's principal clothing towns. Fiennes on the other hand noted it as a neat stone-built village (Morris 1949 17). At the end of our period Collinson described it as a small town (Collinson 1791 iii 370). So we can conclude that it was unusually small for a town but had important non-agrarian functions. Or in the terms Phythian-Adams suggested there were times when it had an urban quality. Had it changed since the Middle Ages? Its lords, the priory of Hinton, obtained a charter for a fair in 1255 and subsequently had the number of days extended. However, its entry in 1327 was not impressive. It had only one occupational byname of a non-rural character and its nine payers contributed sums ranging from 6d to 3s giving a total wealth of £14 10s. By 1334 this had increased to £15. Then in 1345 the monks had their fair at Hinton transferred to Norton (Hulbert 1936 89-91). They provided the George Inn (*50*) to serve these fairs. We know that the monks of Bath complained about the fairs as damaging to their economic interests. Also Shaw points out that the drapers of Bristol regarded the May fair at Norton as one of the 'general fairs' that is one of the eight main regional events (Shaw 993 87-9). So things probably improved after the transfer. Also it should be remembered that if a bustling market was not reflected in taxable wealth, a major fair was even less likely to be. Instead it allowed the merchants of Bristol and perhaps those from further away to share in the business. Thus it seems that late medieval Norton St Philip was always small but economically significant and at times busy. Its status will be discussed further in Chapter 5.

Parallels to Norton can be found elsewhere in England. In Worcestershire Christopher Dyer produced a classification which should seem largely familiar from previous discussions. At the top was Worcester, classed as a large town. It had between 3,000 and 4,000 inhabitants and was larger than any Somerset town. Then came larger market towns, small market towns, non-urban boroughs (in other words places with a borough constitution which failed to develop a lasting urban economy and in terms used here abortive or failed towns) and villages with markets. But in addition he recognised 'informal centres of trades and crafts that grew during the later middle ages'. There were two of these, Redditch

THE GEORGE, NORTON ST PHILLIPS.

50 Norton St Philip. The grand George Inn records both the importance of the fair and the investment the monks of Hinton Charterhouse were willing to put into its promotion. Besides providing food and accommodation it acted as a warehouse at fair time. The fair was held on the field to its rear between the George and the church

and King's Norton. Both were located in the north of the county where a combination of livestock farming and rural industry ensured a buoyant economy after the Black Death. In the same area Stourbridge was another latecomer but had the attributes of a full market town (C. Dyer 2000b 4-6). Norton St Philip is obviously of the same period but has rather more formal origins due to the monks' activities in consolidating their fairs and building the splendid George Inn as associated accommodation.

Turning to the fortunes of the undoubted towns, there was again considerable variety. Wells continued to evolve as a centre for the local gentry. Already during the Commonwealth when the Corporation acquired (temporarily as it turned out) the canonical house in the Market Place they converted it to a 'public room and house for the reception of the country at the time of the assize and sessions' (HMC *Wells* ii 431). The atmosphere of the town during the assizes was captured by Celia Fiennes half a century later. She found the inns full and the streets lined with stalls (Morris 1949 242). In the intervening years there had been the first signs of a new genteel social life. A music club was set up, with a local physician, Claver Morris, as one of the leading members (Hobhouse 1934). Later, during the eighteenth century, assembly rooms and a small theatre were added (Bailey 1982 127; SRO DD/WM 56). These facilities were much smaller scale than those at Bath and aimed at local users, whereas Bath came to cater for the social and leisure needs of the affluent across the nation. This active social life and concentration of those who were comfortably resourced (although not very rich) did not entirely benefit Wells traders. The affluent were now more mobile. Claver Morris' journal is full of travels not only for professional reasons but with friends for pleasure and visits. It is also striking that he did so much shopping elsewhere. Clothes or materials to make them came from London or Bristol, glass and metal goods from Bristol, while books and the ornamental urns for his house came from Bath. In addition his large orders of wines and spirits were smuggled. They came up from the Dorset coast and were frequently delivered at night.

Towards the bottom of the hierarchy, Watchet stabilised its position by the 1680s when it became the main port for coal imports from south Wales into Somerset. It thus specialised, leaving cattle imports and passenger traffic to Minehead (*VCH* v 159).

1686, THE SURVEY OF INNS

The Army had experienced problems in accommodating both its men and their horses during Monmouth's rebellion. As a result the authorities undertook a survey of inns and alehouses to establish what was available (PRO WO 30/48). The result is a useful window on towns at this time of transition both in their numbers and roles.

Generally one can expect that the larger and busier the town the more visitors it would attract and therefore that more accommodation would be available. Also this is a significant time to look at inns as their role had changed with alterations in marketing and communications. Everitt sums it up well, writing: 'The Elizabethan and Stuart inn has no exact counterpart in the modern world. It was the hotel, the bank, the warehouse, the exchange, the scrivener's office and the market place of many a private trader' (Everitt 1967 559-61). Fewer deals were being done in the open market and more people were travelling for business reasons. Both activities focused on the larger inns. In addition they were assuming wider functions. All this is illustrated by the journal of Claver Morris. He regularly sat on two official commissions, respectively for the Land Tax and the Sewers. He was also involved in a short-lived commission for the enclosure of Glastonbury commons. The Commission for Sewers met in the assize hall at Wells but the others met in inns and even the Sewer Commissioners regularly concluded business by dining at an inn. Morris also visited another inn about the selection of a jury. His journal, which covers the period 1684 to 1726, also records him dining, drinking, holding meetings of his music society, reading the news, exerting election pressure, undertaking land transfers and seeing a play at the many inns in Wells. Interestingly he only once visited one for professional reasons when he went to the Fountain to prescribe for a dragoon although Hobhouse suggested that he might have seen patients in the considerable periods of time he spent at the Crown and Christopher inns.

Before discussing what the survey tells us about Somerset towns it is necessary to consider its nature as a source. To begin, it is incomplete. Somerset has over 400 parishes but the survey lists 347 places and these include small settlements that are part of a wider parish. Some are well-established hamlets, such as Sea and Green Ore, but others are more obscure, for example Boardon Bridge or Shurdish Gold Ball, which seem to be attempts to locate isolated alehouses with a few beds on some route. So there are substantial gaps and these seem concentrated in the north and south of the county. In the south the towns of Milborne Port and Yeovil are omitted although the former was found in the Dorset returns. In the north the gaps are larger. Another of the towns we have been studying, Keynsham, is missing but also the neighbouring village of Saltford. Further west along the estuary all of Pill, Portishead, Clevedon and, probably, the Gordano villages are omitted. There are occasional absences elsewhere. In the far west Dulverton is missing. There are also ambiguities. Which is the village identified as Weston? Similarly we have two places merely called Compton and only Compton Martin clearly differentiated. It is assumed that the entry for Stowey relates to Nether Stowey as Over Stowey is listed separately.

Figure *51* lists all places with ten or more guest spaces, and when more than

1. Wells	402	(599)
2. Bath	324	(451)
3. Taunton	247	(265)
4. Bridgwater	143	(246)
5. Chard	91	(342)
6. Glastonbury	91	(45)
7. Bruton	72	(142)
8. Wellington	64	(58)
9. Bishop's Lydeard	60	(48)
10. Minehead	59	(28)
11. Crewkerne	54	(130)
12. Wiveliscombe	53	(76)
13. Wincanton	50	(254)
14. Somerton	44	(78)
15. Ilminster	39	(122)
16. Shepton Mallet	39	(108)
17. Ilchester	38	(83)
18. Dunster	37	(74)
19. Norton St Philip	35	(90)
20. Castle Cary	29	(54)
21. Frome	29	(35)
22. Stogumber	29	(15)
23. Milverton	27	(28)
24. Axbridge	24	(86)
25. Milborne Port	24	(32)
26. South Petherton	24	(15)
27. Pensford	20	(102)
28. Langport	18	(34)
29. Langford	17	(38)
30. Croscombe	16	(16)
31. Nether Stowey	15	(16)
32. Watchet	15	(15)
33. Weare	13	(60)
= Wrington	13	(60)
35. Williton	13	(6)
36. Martock	12	(24)
37. Stack (?)	12	(8)
38. Chewton Mendip	11	(38)
39. North Petherton	11	(21)
40. Comor (?)	11	(20)
41. Stogursey	11	(7)
42. Huntspill	10	(22)

Figures in brackets stable space for horses

51 Facilities at inns in 1686 (all places with over 10 guest beds ranked)

one place has the same number of beds stabling has been used to establish rank order. This longer list has been selected to help illustrate any new centres and to prepare for the discussion of service villages in the next chapter. There was a point of difficulty with Taunton as there are two successive entries with that name. The larger is used in the table while the smaller involved only 15 beds and stabling for 28 horses. There are two possible explanations. Firstly, the entries might reflect the two parishes in the town. This seems unlikely in that other towns with more than one parish, Bath and Glastonbury, are not divided. Also, were this the reason, one would have expected a more equal division. Secondly, the smaller number may reflect inn capacity at those portions of St Mary's and St James' parishes lying beyond the town limits. As this seems more likely they have been omitted from fig. *51*. However, their inclusion would have not altered Taunton's position in the rankings and only slightly changed the gaps between it and the towns on either side.

To put the table in context, Bristol had 1,019 beds and stables for 1,377 horses. Apart from Milborne Port abstracted from the Dorset entries, 41 places are listed out of the 347 in the survey. Of the remainder, 72 had no guest beds and 234 (67 per cent of the whole) had between one and nine. It should also be noted that while the list reflects the importance of towns, it also reflects other things. The most obvious is relationship to the transport network. This is clearly seen by the provision at Langford and Weare, villages on opposite sides of Mendip. They clearly had facilities to enable travellers to eat, spend the night, rest or change their horses before or after crossing the hills.

Typically the ratio of beds to stables is between about one-and-a-half and two to one. When the ratio is higher places are generally on a main route. This is strikingly obvious at Chard with 91 beds and 342 stables or Wincanton with 50 beds and 254 stables both of which were on the London–Exeter road. Conversely places with a low proportion of stables were places where arrivals were going to stay rather than pause in a journey. At Bath with a ratio of 1:1.39 visitors included those using the baths. At Minehead, with a majority of beds people had to wait for ships or for the right wind and tide for them to sail.

Turning to the table, Wells is by a considerable margin the best provided. This must reflect its growing role as a social centre for the gentry and the attractions of business at the cathedral, assize and quarter sessions. Next is Bath which is obviously important but was not yet experiencing the major boom for visitors. Predictably these are followed by Taunton and Bridgwater. These four are clearly in a different class to all the others. Together they have more guest accommodation than the other 38 listed in fig. *51*.

Bruton ranks seventh with Chard and Glastonbury above it. This second is something of a surprise given that Fiennes, about a decade later, dismissed it as 'now a poor ragged place' (Morris 1949 242). Not for the first time we find our evidence disagreeing. A possible part of the answer lies in the time taken to develop a major inn and attract a clientele. In other words there was an element of inertia in the system. This would explain the dominance of Wells when its economy had weakened. There six of its major inns can be dated to at least the fifteenth century and another three are first mentioned in the first decade of the sixteenth century. In 1606 some 16 inns were prosecuted for selling short measure and no less than 13 of them were described as 'ancient'. Inertia would also explain the low provision at Frome despite the growth then underway. So Glastonbury may have been boosted by past affluence which had equipped it with its fine George Inn.

The list continues, largely showing towns in a predictable order (but for the moment ignoring other places such as Langford). Thus Wellington follows Bruton and Stogursey is near the bottom. A few are worthy of comment. Ilminster is relatively lowly placed at 15. This could be a sign that its great days were over. However, it is probably due to a combination of other factors. It was away from the two main routes into Devon passing respectively through Crewkerne and Chard or Taunton and Wellington, so it would not have had the demand from passing travellers. It also lacked higher level administrative, judicial or ecclesiastical functions to draw periodic visitors. Again its social distribution of wealth suggests a market for ale houses rather than fully fledged inns. Lastly there is the issue of inertia. Provision may not have caught up with its improved status. In contrast Ilchester is well placed at 17. Its inns probably reflect its superior position at a focus of main roads rather than any economic recovery. They can also be related to the comment that brewing was the only industry the town maintained in the seventeenth century (*VCH* iii 189). Nether Stowey is again higher than might be expected on previous performance. This probably reflects a combination of its position on the road to Minehead and the attempt to revive its market.

To conclude on the generally recognised towns and failed medieval towns it should be remembered that Dulverton, Keynsham and Yeovil are missing from the survey. Two other places are included but had less than the ten beds that formed the threshold (*51*). They are Stoford and Montacute, which had respectively three and six guest beds. Such numbers do not differentiate them from the county's villages.

What of the other places included in the table? Only Norton St Philip performs outstandingly amongst the possible new foundations. Most of the others do not appear in the list and have little in the way of accommodation for travellers (*54*). That leaves some 10 others. Several are sites on main routes, such as Langford. Others are service villages. Martock seems a good example. It was a large village and the centre of its hundred. It was granted a fair as early as 1247.

This returned a modest 6s 8d profit in 1302. Thereafter Hulbert could only find records of survival as a pleasure fair (Hulbert 1936 136-7). It also had a market with a cross and later a market hall. However, the market was intermittent, having been discontinued in the seventeenth and early eighteenth centuries but revived in 1753 (*VCH* iv 99). Wrington seems broadly similar as regards size, market and fair (but see further discussion on both in Chapter 5).

There remains an area of doubt. Why is Bishop's Lydeard placed ninth with 60 beds and stabling for 48 horses? It is less than 5 miles (8km) from Taunton and even closer to Milverton. It is thus badly placed to offer more than minimal services to either locals or travellers. The apparent anomaly is increased when it is realised that two other places respectively 7 miles (11km) and 10 miles (16km) to the north-west also possessed exceptional facilities. They are Stogumber with 29 beds and Williton with 13. The three are sited along the vale between the Quantock and Brendon Hills. They are therefore along a line of movement north from Taunton to the ports of west Somerset. But there was a choice of route along the east or west of the valley which meant that they might be missed, particularly Stogumber if travellers went by Crowcombe and Bicknoller instead. In fact Williton has what seems the more promising site where the road from Taunton to Watchet crossed that from Bridgwater to Minehead. None of them was outstanding in its wealth. In 1334 Williton was worth £45, Bishop's Lydeard £23 and Stogumber with neighbouring Preston a mere £9 15s. By 1581-2 Bishop's Lydeard had improved to £222. Williton was £169 and Stogumber £46. Bishop's Lydeard and Stogumber had fairs but not Williton. Bishop's Lydeard's fair dated from 1281 and Stogumber's was in being by 1337. (Hulbert 1936 145-6). Then in the seventeenth century there was an attempt to improve the status of Stogumber. Sir John Sydenham bought a Saturday market of the Crown in 1615. This may have been based on some existing activity, as a shambles was recorded in the previous year. By 1637 the market was worth £13 rent. But a market hall was not provided until *c.*1800 (*VCH* v 186).

This modest level of activity hardly justifies the provision of as many beds as were found at Castle Cary and Frome. In the absence of other obvious explanations in Stogumber or the other two places and their route ways, perhaps they should be related to a tendency for places around the fringe of Exmoor and the Brendon Hills to have generous capacity at their inns as fig. *52* shows. For example, Wiveliscombe had as many as 53 beds, placing it 12th in the county and even little Porlock only just missed inclusion in fig. *51* with nine beds. So the answer may lie in patterns of exploitation and movement on these uplands.

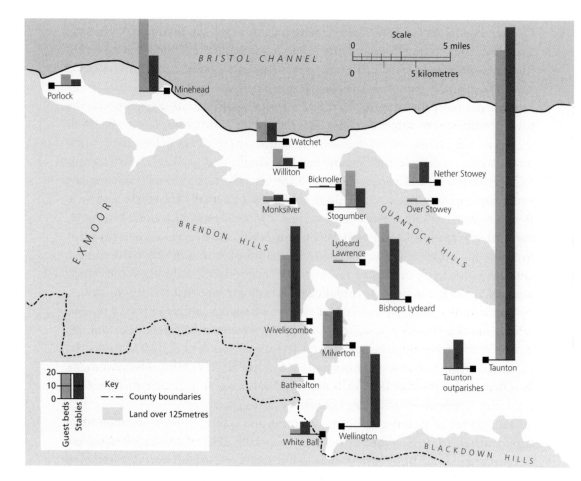

52 Capacity of inns around the Western Hills 1686

THE EIGHTEENTH CENTURY

Despite the presence of Bath and Wells, other towns began to provide housing aimed at the gentry or would-be gentry. The Duke of Chandos' development of the castle site at Bridgwater from 1724 is an early and important example (*VCH* vi 200). Gentry interests also intensified in the seven towns that each returned two MPs as families tried to establish or maintain their influence over elections. By about 1730 the Dodingtons controlled one Bridgwater seat by reason of local estates and customs interests. The other was shared by the Lords Egmont, the Tyntes, Pouletts, Percivals and Balches. The Luttrells controlled Minehead and the Lockyers Ilchester. The Medlycotts and Walters shared Milborne Port. The Wyndhams usually controlled one seat at Taunton. In contrast Bath was independent. Wells also initially gave scope for competition although the Cowards had enough influence to secure the election of two successive William

Cowards, father and son, and for a time the second's son-in-law the Hon. George Hamilton. But from the mid-century the Tudways were able to use the wealth of their Antigua plantation to make the city their pocket borough (Dunning 1983 78).

After the reorganisation of the cloth industry in the late seventeenth century, town fortunes were subject to the usual sort of variations. The attempt to revive the market functions of Nether Stowey and Milborne Port achieved no long-term change. Bruton lost its wealthy resident family. The Berkeley fortunes never fully recovered from the sequestration of the Civil War. In 1698 the manor house was temporarily lost due to a mortgage default. Eventually the house passed to the Hoares in 1776. They never lived there and in the following decade had its size reduced (*VCH* vii 24-5). In contrast Bridgwater was diversifying. Lord Chandos' investments in the town were not limited to housing. He also introduced soap and glass making (*VCH* vi 222). The former failed but glass works persisted until mid-century. Lord Chandos' glass house was then converted to manufacturing pottery and tiles. This exploitation of the local clays was already apparent in 1709 when a brick kiln was established at Hemp (Dunning 1992 60-1). Subsequently it led to the establishment of a large brick works. A more locally based enterprise maintain prosperity at Langport in the late eighteenth century and afterwards. It was provided by the firm of Stukey and Bagehot and more particularly by successive generations of Stukeys (*VCH* iii 26).

Another set of changes in both marketing and transport were apparent from about mid-century. As regards marketing, the great days of the inns had passed. Fewer transactions took place within them and more specialised outlets such as coffee shops began to erode their functions. Wells probably had a tobacconist by 1730 and certainly had a coffee shop in 1732 (SRO DD/TD Box 30/28 & DD/CC 13202). They occupied prime sites in respectively the eastern part of High Street and Sadler Street. In the second half of the century the town lost four long-existing inns (Scrase 1984 385-6). All had also been on commercially attractive sites: the Three Kings on the eastern part of High Street, the Angel and King's Arms at the eastern end of Chamberlain Street and the Rose and Crown in Sadler Street. Similar conversions can be discovered elsewhere. In Langport the George and White Hart had been converted to houses by 1779 (*VCH* iii 21). In Nether Stowey another George and the Crown vanished at about this time (*VCH* v 192). At Somerton the White Hart was subdivided before 1786 (*VCH* iii 132).

Moving on to transport, we are now in the stagecoach era and town authorities were forced to look to issues of accessibility. They had two areas of concern; access to their town and movement within it. The former gave rise to the creation of turnpike trusts. Bath was a pioneer with the Bath Turnpike Act of 1707. Taunton and Wells followed later in the century. These larger towns were then able to entrench their positions by ensuring that the better roads focused on them. This subsequently led to an uneconomic profusion of trusts, particularly in the south of the country where even Martock possessed its own. As a result roads periodically changed hands. Thus the London–Exeter road at Crewkerne was taken over by a Chard-based trust in 1753. A Crewkerne Trust was established in 1765 and in 1810 it took over the Exeter road (*VCH* iv 5-7).

Within towns, improvements generally date to after 1750. When they began to act, the Somerset towns had the example of Bristol to follow. That city had undertaken its first road widening (on the approaches to Bristol Bridge) as early as 1678. In the new century it began to act vigorously against encroachments on the highway and in 1727 the Corporation removed the Corn Market which had been erected in the middle of Wine Street in 1623 (Scrase 1999 29-30). Then in 1733 it removed its High Cross and in 1738 the first of its medieval gates was demolished. During this period Bath was involved in one small improvement although it was concerned with pedestrian circulation rather than wheeled vehicles. The problem was occasioned by the rise of a fashionable leisure area to the east of the Abbey Church around the Orange Grove. Unfortunately the most direct approach was through the length of the church. So Wade's Passage was created to its north. This was easily achieved. One property was involved, it was Corporation owned and the tenant was an alderman (Fawcett and Inskip 1994 35). In 1750 Gloucester joined in obtaining an Improvement Act which led progressively to the clearing of churches, houses and halls from Westgate, Southgate and Northgate Streets together with the High Cross at their junction (Herbert 1988 162).

From 1750 the towns of Somerset began to act, sweeping away middle rows in streets and squares and clearing town gates where they existed. From 1770 it was increasingly common to remove High Crosses as well. Besides questions of access by vehicles, councillors were also concerned with ideas of banishing what were now seen as unseemly uses, particularly the slaughtering of animals, and of improving the townscape to accord with the more regular ideas of Georgian design.

The first to attempt 'improvements' were Bath and Wells in 1754. The former removed the town's north and south gates. Wells Corporation was more ambitious. High Street was cleared of all of its middle row, stalls and its butchering. Two properties on the north of the street were purchased. They were redeveloped creating a yard behind them where the displaced functions were housed. Bath then resolved to tackle the northern entry to the town where High Street was congested by stalls and the seventeenth-century guildhall. It was proposed to build a new guildhall and a market hall on the east side of the street. In contrast to Wells this could not be done by agreement so an Improvement

Act was obtained in 1766. The scheme then took many years to implement. The guildhall was not finished until 1777 (Scrase 1999 55-7). In Taunton the key to improvement was the creation of Market Trustees in 1768. In 1772 they cleared the market place at the south end of Fore Street of the medieval guildhall, the market house of 1682 with its assembly rooms above, 11 other buildings and the High Cross (Bush 1975 19).

While all this was going on, Bristol had moved on to more street widening but also cutting new streets through the old irregular urban mass. The initial impetus came with the actions of the Bridge Trustees to rebuild the bridge and improve access to it (Scrase 1999 34). Taunton was the first Somerset town to obtain a new street; this was Hammet Street of 1788 (*29*). It ran from the market place straight to the tower of St Mary Magdalene's church. Previously this had been accessed only by narrow Great and Little Magdalene Lanes. It was a piece of civic design rather than a traffic artery, having been financed (and named after) an aspiring MP (Scrase 1999 34-6). Bath had more serious problems to resolve. Access was poor both to and between the various baths. In addition links were poor between the medieval centre and the fashionable upper town. After six years debate a further Improvement Act was obtained. It established Commissioners empowered to rebuild the pump room and provide five new roads. Only Bath Street was built in the eighteenth century and the full scheme was never finished.

While all of this was going on, Wells had from 1779 been concerned with the area around Market Place. The corporation seems to have become aware that the economic status of the town was declining. This had focused their attention on improving facilities for marketing. Now they faced a further threat. The assizes and quarter sessions met in the market house initially provided by Bishop Knight and rebuilt or refurbished after 1660. The courts were protected from the weather and the bustle of the market only by screens. The judges and magistrates were dissatisfied and threatened to move. After trying to obtain funds from the county the Corporation had to embark on a major scheme. The canonical house on the south side of Market Place was purchased. Its front garden was thrown into the Market Place and a new town hall erected beyond. This had space for the courts and was initially open at ground-floor level to accommodate the cheese market. Subsequently, the market area was further tidied by removal of the High Cross and Bekynton's Conduit (Scrase and Hasler 2002 15, 27, 147-51 & 216-7).

All these trends of road clearance, road creation and market improvement were to continue into the nineteenth century. It is also striking that existing systems of town government were either unable to tackle problems or were not trusted. The immediate result was the creation of bodies of commissioners or trustees, but major reform was to follow.

However, for Somerset at large, the major change came in the last years of the eighteenth century when competition from the Lancashire cotton and Yorkshire woollen industries largely destroyed west-country spinning and weaving. Collinson reported the crisis in Somerset. At Milverton the production of serges and druggets was much declined. In the country around Keynsham they were 'now entirely dropt'. At Pensford the production of cloth was 'dreadfully decayed' and 'bereft of trade many of the houses are fallen into ruins' (Collinson 1791 ii 400 ,429 & iii 13). A number of places such, as Taunton as early as the 1770s (Bush 1975 58), and later Bruton had switched to silk production which was to sustain them into the next century but there was deep dislocation.

There were other changes. Barry, writing of the whole south-west region, refers to the balance shifting away from the smaller places. In Somerset he calculated that only 28 of his suggested 36 towns in 1673 were constantly recorded as towns in the period 1600 to 1800 and five of these were of marginal significance (*CUH* ii 73 & 85). Patterns of demand, distribution and changes in transport systems were all working to smaller places' disadvantage. We have seen one example of this in the emergence of turnpike trusts based in the larger towns. Figure 53 shows the results of all this. Dunster, Langport and Axbridge have joined Milborne Port, Ilchester and Nether Stowey at a population of 1,000 or less and lacking the size now proper for urban status. The Stukey family helped to keep Langport prosperous but the others were less fortunate. Stogursey's population is misleading, reflecting the appearance of flourishing hamlets in the parish. It had long ceased to be a town. Minehead and Dulverton were in little better state. The former had lost the Irish short sea crossing traffic to Holyhead. They too were of doubtful viability as towns. Most of these nine were to feel their decline, as nineteenth-century reforms would deprive those that possessed them first of MPs and then municipal corporations.

There are a number of other changes shown (53). Yeovil had grown strikingly now its old rivals had all collapsed. Shepton Mallet, Wellington, Chard and Crewkerne had all improved. In contrast, Wells had slipped back in relative terms. In an age when strong urban growth was common, it had barely increased since 1642. It may have had a settled, comfortable way of life but it did not attract new enterprises or settlers.

So we end with the old order changing. The nineteenth century was going to intensify the changes. The early possession of main-line railway links would have dramatically altered fortunes. Then the rise of seaside resorts would make further changes, adding new towns and reviving some older foundations, notably Minehead. However, that story is beyond the scope of this work.

1. Bath	31,496
2. Frome	9,493
3. Taunton	6,997
4. Bridgwater	4,911
5. Shepton Mallet	4,638
6. Wellington	3,874
7. Yeovil	3,118
8. Crewkerne	3,021
9. Chard	2,932
10. Wells	2,923
11. North Petherton	2,615
12. Glastonbury	2,337
13. Ilminster	2,160
14. South Petherrton	1,867
15. Wincanton	1,850
16. Keynsham	1,748
17. Watchet	1,659
18. Milverton	1,637
19. Bruton	1,536* (1,746)
20. Somerton	1,478
21. Castle Cary	1,406
22. Stogursey	1,208
23. Minehead	1,037
24. Dulverton	1,035
25. Milborne Port	1,000
26. Dunster	868
27. Langport	861
28. Montacute	857
29. Axbridge	835
30. Ilchester	818
31. Nether Stowey	620
32. Pensford	296

* town only, parish in brackets

53 Population from the 1811 census

CHAPTER 5

MICRO-TOWNS OR SERVICE VILLAGES

THE BOTTOM OF THE HIERARCHY

Clark employed the term 'micro-town' to describe places with a population of less than 800 at the end of the seventeenth century which nevertheless performed urban functions *(CUH* ii 736). This coinage illustrates the difficulties of drawing a line at the bottom of the hierarchy of towns. Elsewhere in the *Cambridge Urban History of Britain* Christopher Dyer wrote: 'Drawing a dividing line through the rather fuzzy categories of very small market towns, market villages and industrial villages leaves the historian with few easy choices' *(CUH* i 511).

Sometimes it is, of course, straightforward, particularly with failed towns. Where a medieval foundation has vanished and there are only some combination of bumps in a field, an unusual pattern of boundaries and occasional documentary references there is no problem. Again the issues are simple if the place has shrunk to a hamlet as with Lower Weare or a small village as at Nether Stowey. There is more difficulty if a place remains large and thus generates more functions that what would be regarded as a typical village. It becomes ever more complicated if the place sometimes exhibited urban features but lost them in hard times, as at Watchet or Milborne Port.

This problem of demarcation is even more acute when one is trying to distinguish between a small town and a large or multifunction village. The discussions that have gone before have tried to highlight these issues in two ways. Firstly, the views of Leland and Gerard have been contrasted with our own. Secondly, particular attention has been paid to the examples of Pensford and Norton St Philip. Both always seem to have been small but they have displayed a range of functions. Early modern writers except Fiennes regarded both as towns but modern commentators have included Pensford in their lists of towns but not

Norton. This differentiation seems the more questionable given the latter's major fair and Leland's comments on the two.

It is suggested that we tend to put too much emphasis on size both in terms of population and physical extent. Early modern writers were more concerned with function. This does not mean that population should be disregarded. Clark points out that Blome in 1673 identified 142 flourishing and 94 mean towns. He then calculated that the flourishing towns had an average population of 1,030 while the mean towns' average only 560 (*CUH* ii 736). Urban fortunes certainly related to size but we should not promote it to being the prime consideration or set too high a threshold. Similarly, in considering the functional divide we may confuse ourselves by expecting too sharp a division. Towns are often seen as providing goods and services for a catchment area of greater or lesser extent. Villages in contrast are settlements of the local agricultural population with only such crafts as they need, for example a blacksmith and miller.

In fact, reality is more complicated. Medieval and early modern Somerset possessed a number of small settlements with roles other than farming. To begin with there were those with some sort of harbour facility on the coast or navigable rivers. They extended from Pill on the Avon in the north to Porlock and Minehead in the west and included now almost forgotten facilities such as Lilstock (Aston 1985 140). All would have seen the movement of goods to and from the surrounding area. Also there would have been the opportunity for different types of employment such as fishing, smuggling, shipbuilding and piloting (the last a specialism at Pill). Next there were manufacturing villages. Croscombe was a good example in the early days of the cloth industry which left it some substantial houses, a handsome village cross and a well-endowed chantry (Green 1888 311; Woodward 1982 5). Thirdly, there were places offering facilities to travellers on main roads. The pace of travel dictated regular stops where travellers could obtain a meal, spend the night or (in the coaching era) change their horses. There were a few places where mining or quarrying was important. Finally, there were places with a market or fair. These last are often called service villages.

The problem is deciding what from this list was required to make a town either in the view of past commentators or for our own studies. Certainly, one of these features would not be enough. The other late medieval general or regional fairs in northern Somerset besides those at Norton St Philip were the St Andrew's and St Calixtus' fairs at Wells and those at Priddy and Queen's Charlton (Shaw 1993 87-8). These last two places were no more than hamlets and nobody ever seems to have described them as towns. Similarly, nobody styled Croscombe a town even at its period of great prosperity. Even two such functions might not serve. Martock was a large village with a small fair and a market but once again was never described as anything else except by Collinson (Collinson 1791 iii

2). In contrast Pensford and Norton St Philip with manufacturing, marketing and major facilities for travellers at a convenient first stop south of, respectively, Bristol and Bath, were regularly described as towns. Norton's fair added more weight to its classification.

Inevitably some preliminary sorting has been necessary before the detailed assessments which follow. Generally, villages with a fair, market or both have been excluded if nobody ever referred to them as a town and their tax profiles do not distinguish them from other villages. Compton Dundon is an example. The lady of the manor, Cecilia de Vivonne, obtained the grant of a market and fair in 1289 (Collinson 1791 iii 447; Hulbert 1936 139). The site was presumably where the road linking the two elements of the settlement, Compton and Dundon, crossed the main road from Glastonbury to Somerton. It is still marked by a somewhat restored cross. Nevertheless, the place seems to have remained a village and any little passing trade vanished early.

In addition, places mentioned as a town by one or both of Leland and Collinson have sometimes been omitted. This is because they were freer with the term than others and it is felt that the discussions of Cannington and Chew Magna below are sufficient to cover this group. The most prominent of those excluded is Cheddar. Leland called it 'a good husband tounlet to Axbridge', which perhaps implies some degree of complementarity in the functions and timing of markets, while Collinson uses the term town without his usual addition of market. In fact he refers to a former considerable market which had ceased to function over a century before although the two livestock fairs survived. What seems to have impressed him was size and the level of manufacturing. He refers to the manufacture of paper and the spinning and knitting of hose (Toulmin Smith 1964 iv 143; Collinson 1791 iii 572). However, tax returns are not impressive. Indeed in 1581-2 there were 23 payers on land out of a total of 48.

This issue of where to draw the line is critical for the whole south-west region. Clark estimates that *c.*1670 the region had 76.9 per cent of its small towns with a population of 900 or less, a further 18.8 per cent with populations between 901 and 1,800 and a mere 4.3 per cent with between 1,801 and 2,750 inhabitants. The next most dense concentration of these small places was in the north-west, with 69.4 per cent of 900 or less. At the opposite extreme the East Midlands had only 54.2 per cent (*CUH* ii 738). So our next task is to review the marginal places and attempt some differentiation.

ASSESSING POSSIBLE MICRO-TOWNS

The places considered here are those mentioned in the discussions above as being from time to time described as towns together with two others. Firstly there is North Curry which also features in early modern town lists. Then there is Stogumber discussed in the previous chapter. These are more commonly classified as service villages today. In the past Stogumber was rarely called a town. Figure 54 shows statistics on the places to be discussed plus material on small towns in Gloucestershire for comparison. This Gloucestershire group includes a place Leland described as a townlet (Wickwar) and another he classified as an *uplandische* town (Fairford).

A preliminary inspection reveals that our information has many gaps. To begin, Chew Magna is omitted except in relation to the 1563 diocesan survey (which was done by ecclesiastical parishes) and the 1686 survey of inns. Although the name appears in other records as that of a hundred, the division into tithings within the hundred disguises the actual settlement. As a result, no other figures can be given until the nineteenth-century censuses. Others have gaps. The problems with Pensford have already been discussed. Mells frequently appears in unhelpful forms. In 1334 it paid on wealth of £70 but there was a further element included in the lump sum paid by the abbot of Glastonbury. In 1581-2 payments are made for the combined manors of Mells and Leigh. Similarly the 1558 and 1581-2 payments for Norton St Philip are combined returns for Norton and Hinton. Stogumber is not named in 1327 and in 1334 it was assessed with the hamlet of Preston.

As will become apparent, five of the places under consideration were the centre of a hundred that was named after them. So some consideration of the relationship of hundreds and urban development is necessary. In fact 11 of our medieval towns were similarly the titular centre of a hundred. They were places that were at Domesday either boroughs or centres of royal manors, plus the ecclesiastical centre of Wells. However, not all Anglo-Saxon towns had their own hundred. Axbridge and Langport which, as has been explained, were away from the manorial centre, were excluded but so were Ilchester and Milborne Port. Predictably the foundations of the twelfth and thirteenth centuries, for example Bridgwater and Chard, arrived too late to alter the established pattern of hundreds. Many hundreds came to have a single town such as Wincanton in Norton Ferris hundred or Chard in East Kingsbury hundred but some hundreds were entirely rural, for example Coker, Hartcliffe and Portbury. In contrast, a few hundreds had several towns (55). This was particularly so with the large hundreds of the upland west and those of the over-provided south. In the former Carhampton hundred contained both Dunster and Minehead while Williton hundred had Dulverton, Nether Stowey and Watchet. In the south Tintinhull contained both Ilchester and Montacute. As this implies, hundreds varied in size and the richness of their territory. Small hundreds characterised the south of the county, with units such as Coker, Barwick and Stone. This was also the area of

a. Wealth

Place	1327	1334	1581-2	1641
Cannington	£7-10s- 0d	£19-10s	£34	£44
Chewton Mendip	£88- 6s- 8d	£90	£197	£95
Martock	£80- 0- 0d	£51	£36	£49
Mells	£122- 0s- 0d	£70*	?	£44
North Curry	£30-13s- 6d	£55	£67	?
Norton St Philip	£14-10s- 0d	£15	?	£28
Porlock	£16- 5s-10d	£22-15s	£90	?
Stogumber	?	?	£46	?

* plus an unspecified amount paid direct by the abbot of Glastonbury

b. Inn capacity in 1686

Place	number of beds	stabling
Cannington	6	4
Chew Magna	5	14
Chewton Mendip	11	38
Martock	12	24
Mells	8	12
North Curry	6	11
Norton St Philip	35	90
Pensford	20	102
Porlock	9	5
Stogumber	29	15

c. Population

Place	1563	1642	1811
Cannington*	606	?	1,001 (981)
Chew Magna	848	?	1,527
Chewton Mendip*	924 (545)	?	1,225
Martock	1,025	?	2,356
Mells	505	?	1,061
North Curry	707	1,017	1,346
Norton St Philip	267	?	593
Pensford	303	?	296
Porlock	373	?	633
Stogumber	671	999	1,214

* generally the above are parish figures, township in brackets where available

d. Populations of small towns in southern Gloucestershire for comparison

Place	1563	1603	1676	1811
Chipping Sodbury	45	513	636	1,235
Fairford	136	331	993	1,444
Marshfield	313	844	900	1,415
Wickwar	409	300	420	805
Wotton-under-Edge	580	1,824	5,139	3,800

54 Possible micro-towns

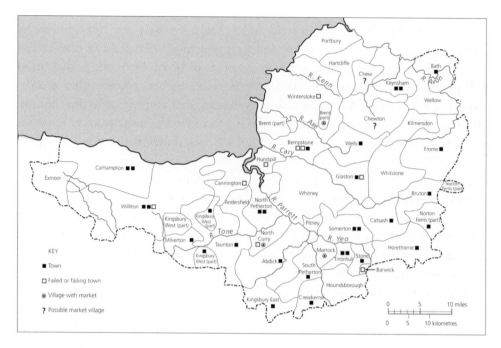

55 The hundreds of Somerset and their towns 1327-34

most intense town foundation although the units do not correspond. So it can be concluded that being the centre of a hundred could confer an advantageous degree of centrality to a settlement but that this did not necessarily occur.

Lastly, as a general remark, it should be noted that the places now under consideration have few of the physical attributes of urbanism apart from, perhaps, a market cross. Patterns are generally undistinguished. Chew Magna and Martock are strung out along the main road of the area. Most of the others are spread along a pattern of branching roads (*60*). None except Norton St Philip (*56*) developed a middle row or island block although Porlock did have its frequent precursors a shambles. Trading either took place in the streets or in some convenient field. The staggered crossroads and possible back lanes at Norton St Philip are alone in hinting at some positive manipulation of pre-existing patterns.

With these limitations in mind we can turn to each place in turn in alphabetic order. Cannington certainly had a possible pedigree for a town in that it was a royal manor at Domesday and the centre of a hundred. However, the recorded wealth and population must be treated with caution in that it was, like many places of this character, a large parish. Until nineteenth-century reforms, it included Combwich with its wharf and ferry across the lower River Parrett (*VCH* vi 73). Even disregarding this, the wealth was not impressive. The best performance relative to other places considered as either certain or possible towns is in 1641. However, over half the wealth in that year was owned by Hugh Rogers esq., who was assessed on land worth £25. In addition Henry Fry, gent, paid on goods worth £4. Cannington would have been larger than most villages and with a rather greater range of functions but it was within 3 miles (5km) of Bridgwater. When the manor passed to the Courcy family they did not promote it as a town but preferred Stogursey which was more than twice as far from Bridgwater. Stogursey remained the only place designated as a borough in the hundred. Also the Courcys obtained a fair there rather than at Cannington. Only Leland in the sixteenth century and Collinson at the very end of our period of study thought Cannington a town. In contrast, the detailed study for the *Victoria County History* discovered an economy based on arable farming. One must conclude that Leland was misled by its size and its having possessed a priory. Similarly while Collinson calls it a town he does not employ his usual formulae of market town or ancient market town which he applied to the places considered in earlier chapters. Probably he was indicating no more than a size greater than the typical village.

Chew Magna was another place that only Leland and Collinson identified as a town. The latter is particularly enthusiastic, writing of it: 'in former days this

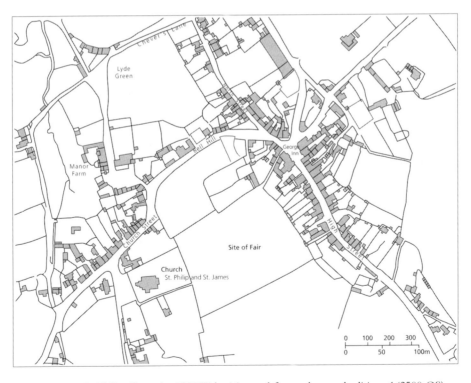

56 Norton St Philip (from the 1838 Tithe Map and first and second editions 1/2500 OS)

was a borough, a market and a large clothing town' (Collinson 1791 ii 94). He then went on to explain that none of these features survived in his own day. Unfortunately, he gave no sources and no confirmation is known for borough status or a market. The patterns revealed on early maps show no sign of the regular plots usually associated with borough creation (57). As mentioned, we lack material to judge these claims in more detail until a thorough modern local study is made. The early twentieth-century account certainly has nothing to suggest urban functions (Wood 1903). Chew Magna seems to have been a larger than average settlement and when Leland wrote it was enjoying a boom in cloth production. Its wealth in the fifteenth and sixteenth centuries seems to be reflected in the church. Money for the north aisle was left in 1443 and the tower (another praised by Pevsner) must have just preceded it (Wood 1903 221-2; Poyntz Wright 1981 100). Pevsner himself associated the tower with a legacy of 1541 (Pevsner 1958 158) but that must have concerned finishing it or some final embellishment. These factors of size and wealth may account for Leland's

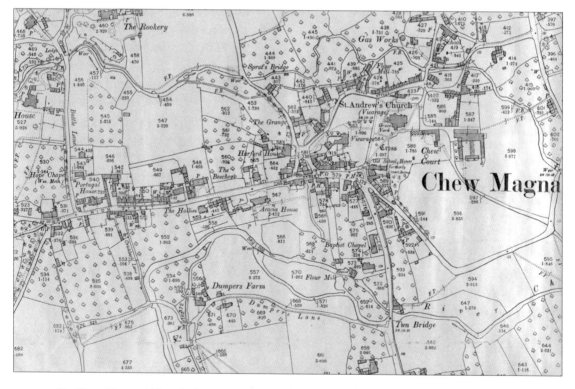

57 Chew Magna. Although there might seem to be a superficial resemblance to Chard (see *12*), if one walks along the main street, the second edition 1/2500 OS reveals the contrast. Here plots vary sharply in form. Many are obviously small individual developments exploiting the road frontage of fields and orchards. Here there is no overall planning

classification. However, it never possessed a fair and had only a churchyard cross.

Chewton Mendip was certainly relatively wealthy and populous (see *54*). It was the centre of a hundred and one of the four centres of the Mendip lead-mining industry. This second must largely explain its prosperity. In turn size and wealth might be expected to draw specialist trades. The 1327 bynames give no sign of this but in 1581-2 there was a need to distinguish two men called Thomas Cole and one is described as the mercer which suggests a demand for more luxurious goods. Again the place had a fair from 1348 (Hulbert 1936 99). All this, and a wealth that was consistently similar to about the tenth-ranked town, does suggest a possible candidate for urban status. In contrast it does less well as regards inns. Eleven guest beds just places it in the higher ranks. However, that number would only indicate a facility serving travellers on a main route. It is significantly less than Langford, which is similarly situated on a main road that is about to climb the slope on to Mendip.

Martock was a royal manor in Domesday and was the centre of its own hundred (although one of the small southern hundreds). It had a medieval fair and market. The market was granted to Ingram de Fiennes in 1247 and the fair was in being by 1302 (*VCH* iv 99). These may represent an attempt at town foundation but most evidence seems to indicate that it operated at a lower level without special status or much diversity of occupation. In 1327 it had one byname suggesting an urban trade: Draper. However, as we have seen it did have fish dealers who travelled as far afield as Exeter. Nevertheless, it seems to lack full urban status. This is understandable as it was within that southern belt where towns clustered together (*41*). Within a 6-mile (9km) radius were all of Ilchester, Yeovil, Montacute, South Petherton and Somerton. It did not flourish after the fourteenth century and in 1581-2 it was one of the very few places with less assessed wealth than in 1327-34. It is unsurprising that the market had vanished by the end of the century. This in turn meant that it did not attract the attention of Blome, Adam and Defoe. It was nevertheless in a rich agricultural area. Gerard commented that it was 'seated in the fattest place of the Earth of the Countie especially for errable which makes ye inhabitants soe fatt in their purses'. This assessment seems to be confirmed by the 1641 return where only 17 people were worth £49. All seemed comfortably placed without any peak or the usual trail of people paying on land worth £1. So it is less surprising that the market was revived in 1753 (*58*), although the economic trends were hardening against smaller places. The stated reason was local dissatisfaction with the facilities and prices at other places (*VCH* iv 99). Subsequently, Collinson described it as 'a large, pleasant market town' (Collinson 1791 iii 2). He was the only commentator to call it a town and, as remarked, he was freer with his use

58 Martock. The eighteenth-century market house with town hall over and the market cross in the form of a Roman Doric column reflect the revival of the market in 1753

of the term than other writers. So Martock might be classified as an intermittent service village just as Nether Stowey could be described as an intermittent town. However, this provokes the question as to whether they differed in anything except the latter's borough status.

Mells was certainly a rich manor although it never had a fair. It was after all Jack Horner's 'plum'. Its wealth, a recent attempt by Abbot Selwood to expand the place, and a thriving cloth industry probably explain why Leland called it a townlet (*59*). Enough of the wealth and the cloth industry survived into the seventeenth century to secure its subsequent mentions as a town. It was located in a hundred (Kilmerston) that otherwise lacked towns. However, its status must have been at best marginal. The fact that only one street was built of Selwood's intended four probably reflects a lack of potential.

North Curry was again the centre for its hundred and a royal manor in Domesday. From Richard I's time it belonged to the dean and chapter of Wells. Its history raises questions as to its relationship with Newport, which was only just over a mile (1.3km) away in the same parish. Indeed, their exact relationship is obscure. The charter granting a weekly market at Newport was issued to

59 Mells. New Street of *c.*1470, the only part built of Abbot Selwood's scheme to transform the settlement. It runs towards the church but does not align with the tower (which is later, being of early sixteenth-century date) or the porch. The combination of these regular terraces and the new tower may explain why Leland thought Mells 'a praty townlet'

Bishop Joscelin but the land belonged to the dean and chapter. Perhaps modern demarcations were less clear to medieval bishops. Certainly Bishop Bekynton financed the building of the New Works in Wells and controlled their form but the site was owned by the dean and chapter apart from a strip at the front taken from the highway. Subsequently, the dean and chapter received the rents. Again, half a century later, Bishop King was a major force in the rebuilding of Bath Abbey. All that is certain here is that the Wells cathedral communar's accounts lack any separate return from Newport.

Could North Curry have taken over functions as Newport failed? In fact the dean and chapter seem to have obtained a market charter from John, a confirmation from Henry III and a further grant from Edward I which added a fair although these are only known from a further charter of Edward III (HMC *Wells* ii charter 252 603). In parallel the bishop's charter for Newport was obtained from King John in 1206. As the North Curry charter from John is only known from later inspections, it is not impossible that they are the same. In which case Edward I's sanction of a switch of market day from Wednesday to Tuesday might coincide with a relocation. However, this seems rather early. As we have seen,

Newport was separately assessed in 1334 and burgages were mentioned there in 1349 and 1384 with out any indication that they were vacant (HMC *Wells* charters 304 & 432 614 & 641; Aston and Leech 1977 115). In addition, the broad road junctions and wide verges which characterise North Curry village suggest that it developed with a market function rather than having one imposed at a relatively late stage (*60*). So the two may well have functioned simultaneously for a time. The chapter's efforts seem like an attempt at town foundation, as does the abbot of Glastonbury's similar actions for Wrington. In both cases the places neither developed a full range of urban specialisms nor collapsed in the manner of Newport, Downend or Weare. Instead, both seem to have continued at a low level of activity. In the eighteenth century a new arrival in the area claimed that his purchase gave him the rights to the fair, market and associated gaol. The profits to the dean and chapter were still sufficient to sting them in to a vigorous defence of their rights (HMC *Wells* ii 505 & 511).

The returns to the dean and chapter are indicated by the communar's accounts. In the earliest surviving, that for 1327-8, the reeve of North Curry paid £165 4s and owed arrears of nearly £59 of which £24 8s 11½d was new and the remainder carried forward from earlier years. It was by far the largest single item of income. The next was £86 12s from Winscombe. The subsequent situation can

60 North Curry from the air. The branching pattern of roads shows no signs of regular pre-planning. However, the wide roads and verges (now often planted with trees) do suggest that the settlement developed with its market. *Courtesy Professor Mick Aston*

be illustrated by sampling the accounts at approximately half-century intervals allowing for gaps in the records of which the largest is from 1347 to 1392. In 1392-3 the reeve paid £160 16s 8d and owed over £82. In 1421-2 the reeve paid £120 and a further £4 was received from the bailiff while arrears were nearly £32. By 1478-9 receipts had fallen to £78 17s 10d. In 1535-5 the accounts were slightly more detailed. The manor paid £76 13s 3¾d and the hundred £3 6s 9d. At this time East Curry and East Lambrook both paid more. By 1587-8 North Curry was once more the best single payment. The manor yielded £129 19s 4d and the hundred a further £5 14s (Colchester 1984). The market would have been included as part of the manor which then provided just over 10 per cent of total income. Unfortunately we have no way of calculating how much of these were attributable to the market and fair. However, the returns of the fair and market were not reflected in any great wealth in the actual settlement judging by subsidy returns, but as we have seen that is a familiar situation.

The problem with North Curry was probably in its location. It is on a low ridge with the wetlands of West Sedge Moor on one side and those of the Tone valley on the other. Taunton was less than 6 miles (9km) on the dry (western) approach and Langport nearly as close on the east although less accessible (*41*).

Norton St Philip has already been discussed at length. It possessed a major late medieval fair and was regularly described as a town in the early modern period. Also like Mells it was located in a hundred (in this case Wellow) which was otherwise without a town. The pattern of development is also interesting. It is basically a staggered crossroads but the form of this stagger is suggestive of deliberate diversions to send all traffic through a market place (*56*). Similarly the existence of what could originally have been back lanes is compatible with an exercise in town foundation by the monks of Hinton Charterhouse. The original nucleus seems to have been to the west around the church, Manor Farm and the two small greens, one by Manor Farm and the other called Lyde Green. In the late seventeenth century, Norton's inns place it 19th in the county ahead of Castle Cary and Frome. All this has to be set against a low population and the limits to wealth in the settlement. However, the sixteenth and seventeenth centuries do show signs of a small prosperous group. As mentioned, the 1558 and 1581-2 returns are confused by the inclusion of Hinton. Nevertheless, something can be made out. In 1558 one payer is noted as being of Hinton. Of the remaining six the richest was John Flower (a family name strongly associated with Norton) who paid on goods worth £20, while another paid on goods worth £10 and three on goods worth £5. This is a strikingly different distribution to normal and indicates a number of affluent people in the area. In 1581-2 nobody is distinguished as being of Hinton and there is a long tail of people paying on the minimum, 14 on goods worth £3 and 10 on land worth

£1. There are only four people paying on goods worth between £6 and £10, including John Flower on £8. Finally in 1641 the return is for Norton only. Payers were few but include Jeffrey Flower who paid on £10 in goods. This was a sum exceeded in no recognised town in Somerset and equalled only in three. Furthermore, it needs to be related to what has been said about the general fall in a typical family's admitted wealth between 1581-2 and 1641. It is also known that Jeffrey Flower was rich enough to pay for the church tower and a considerable amount of other rebuilding to the parish church. He also contributed to the ongoing works at Bath Abbey. He must have been underassessed in at least the same measure demonstrated at Wells.

With Pensford the problems are in some ways similar but more intense. We have no comparative measures of wealth although it performs remarkably well when it can be identified in medieval cloth production or seventeenth-century inns. As regards this last, Pensford, Norton and Stogumber are obviously in a very different class to the other settlements listed in fig. 54. But as with Norton, all these positive features of Pensford have to be set against a small population. Also Pensford differs from Norton in that it has no sign of deliberate creation by a feudal superior. Instead it seems to have evolved through the efforts of individual landholders. They were taking advantage of the assets offered by the River Chew, a bridging point and copious water power (61).

Porlock seems a natural place for a small town. It lies in a valley which is cut off by steep hills; Porlock Hill to the west, Dunkery Beacon to the south and the Mynes and Periton Hill to the east. Within this enclosed territory it had the advantage of a small harbour. However, its population and wealth were always unremarkable and it is only occasionally mentioned as a town. When it is so classed, the reference is often slighting. Gerard found nothing to commend there while Defoe writes of it and Watchet as having been completely displaced by Minehead. Perhaps it had a rustic air to give rise to these comments (62). It did have a fair granted to Nigel Loryng, the lord of the manor, in 1366. By the early modern period this specialised in cattle sales. There was also a weekly cattle market (Hulbert 1936 149-50). This had the common physical expressions of a shambles and a cross.

Stogumber was apparently a small poor place in the fourteenth century. Its wealth of £9 15s with little Preston in 1334 means that it was by a considerable margin the poorest place under consideration here although its substantial church may suggest a different view. It had a fair by 1327 and its profits went to the dean and chapter of Wells. There is less purpose in citing the communar's accounts than with North Curry. Not only is there the problem of knowing whether any other items of income were included but also by 1343 the returns were being farmed. So what we see is an agreed sum for the cathedral while

61 Pensford. The view from the original bridge at Pensford looking toward St Thomas' church. The River Chew flows on the left while a mill leet joins it from the right. A minor stream also came in from the left driving a further wheel. The small churchyard on what is in effect an island reflects the church's origins as a chapel of ease, as burials would have been reserved for the parish church

the farmer would have tried to make as much extra as possible for himself. In 1327, prior to the appointment of a farmer, Stogumber paid £66 13s 4d. From 1343 it paid a sum ranging from £26 to £36 (Colchester 1984). Then in 1614, Sir John Sydenham was granted a market. It is possible that this was a regrant of a lapsed earlier market but it is equally possible that it was a genuine example of a new creation in seventeenth-century Somerset. It was not badly placed. It was within 4 miles (7km) of Watchet but, as we have seen, Gerard dismissed that as a small market at about this time. It was separated from other established towns by both distance and terrain. It may have continued at a fairly low level thereafter. Its return for 1641 is missing but in 1642 it paid £8 16s which was less than neighbouring Bicknoller or Crowcombe. This modest activity seems implicit in the long gap before the provision of a market hall. In contrast, the relatively high population of the parish and its generous inn facilities may suggest rather more success. In 1791 Collinson thought it a small market town (Collinson 1791 iii 545).

This account and earlier discussions on Congresbury, the two Pethertons, Wiveliscombe and Wrington should have illustrated the difficulties to which Dyer referred. We are left with an apparent contradiction. The places with the

62 Porlock. Although it was a minor port and service centre and a significant staging point for those travelling along the coast of north Devon and Somerset, Porlock lacked an urban air. This is apparent even in its main inn. Elsewhere major inns showed their importance by size and impressive facades in some style from the medieval to the Georgian. This was true even of places as small as Pensford and Norton St Philip

most evident urban functions and that were most commonly called towns, Pensford and Norton St Philip, are also the smallest. As regards population it is useful to look beyond Somerset for comparisons. Figure *54d* shows the position for selected places in southern Gloucestershire. The 1563 figures seem remarkably low but even if this is allowed for, Chipping Sodbury, Fairford and Wickwar are of broadly similar size to those places we have been considering. Further afield in Sussex in the sixteenth and seventeenth centuries, no less than eight places with at least some urban pretensions had populations which were never more than around 600 in these two centuries. They included ancient Steyning and two decayed Cinque ports, Seaford and Winchelsea. Kent had another 16 (Clark, Gaskin and Wilson 1989 83-92 & 169-174). Probably the key to what might be regarded as a town depends on the weight given to assessments by contemporaries at various periods that it was a town.

After considering all available data, it is suggested that Pensford and Norton St Philip probably deserve ranking as towns. Certainly they should be treated similarly. At the opposite extreme Cannington was no more than a large village despite Leland. Mells is best described as mainly an industrial village although a surprisingly attractive one by modern standards. Porlock and Martock are probably best classified as service villages. That leaves Chew Magna, Chewton Mendip and North Curry which might be regarded as service villages or small towns. Any decision will depend on both the period under consideration and the criteria to which particular weight is attached. Stogumber is hard to classify. Probably it is unusual for Somerset, being a market created in the seventeenth century.

DISTRIBUTION

It is notable that five of the nine places discussed above (Chew Magna, Chewton Mendip, Mells, Norton St Philip and Pensford) together with two others of doubtful status previously discussed (Congresbury and Wrington) are located on the Mendips or between them and the Avon. This is of course the area influenced by Bristol and to a lesser extent Bath. Now the presence of these two major centres certainly seems to have inhibited the development of fully fledged towns. However, the population of this extensive area could not have walked to Bristol or Bath for more routine requirements. A network of service centres was required. These places undoubtedly fulfilled such a role. Individual fortunes then depended on the state of local industry, the possession of a fair and their position on major routeways.

Again, comparisons with other parts of the country confirm the existence of such patterns. York was another major provincial centre. Like Bristol it had few towns close to it. The nearest, Tadcaster, was over 8 miles (13km) away and the next, Wetherby, 12 miles (19km). In Yorkshire urbanisation was intensifying by the later seventeenth century, but from 1500 to 1650 these two and Boroughbridge (18 miles or 29km from York) all had populations of under 300 (*ibid* 201-2 & 209-10).

CONCLUSIONS

It should be apparent from all this that a continuum of types existed without clear distinctions. The easiest to recognise are those at opposite poles. At the top are towns of medieval foundation that have continued ever since. At the other extreme are places intending to be towns which never achieved urban status. Between we can distinguish a series of possible types. We can begin with what were intended to be towns. Some prospered for a while then faltered and lost their urban features but had them revived when circumstances improved. Watchet, Milborne Port and Nether Stowey are examples of this but differ markedly in their prosperity at their best. Next there are towns that functioned for a time and then failed, for example Stogursey. Then there are places that were intended to be towns but never achieved a full range of urban functions. They did however retain some market functions and continued as service villages. Wrington seems a possible example. Then there were places which were never intended as more than service villages. Again these might be continuous, intermittent or fail subsequently. Martock seems the most likely example and it was intermittent.

CHAPTER 6

CONCLUSIONS

This may have seemed as much a history of tax and tax avoidance as of Somerset towns. Unfortunately this has been inevitable if the various tables were to be interpreted. As we were often relying on taxation records to chart fluctuations in town fortunes, it is important to understand the nature and limitations of the various taxes. It would also have been easy to slip into a detailed history of the West Country textile industry. At least that has been avoided.

From our scrutiny of tax records, two methodological points can be drawn. Firstly, taxes do not give a complete picture but reflect what was being assessed. Medieval levies on movables give a particularly one-dimensional view. Secondly, tax records may give a very different picture to that of contemporaries. Travellers might be struck by the bustle of fairs and markets but this need not be expressed in local wealth. Market trading gave a town a lively air but did not of itself creation fortunes. Also profits could be drawn off to town lords. Fairs could be even less productive as they let merchants from elsewhere tap the local market.

Turning to the towns of Somerset, the main lesson from this study has been the variability of urban fortunes. The most dramatic declines were those of the major Anglo-Saxon centres of Ilchester and Milborne Port but even Bath – which was probably the most consistent high-ranking place – suffered temporary declines notably in the sixteenth century. Obviously a simple linear model is inappropriate. In such a scheme towns are pictured as emerging or being founded and, if they overcome the problems of developing an appropriate role, they are seen as continuing unless some significant event reduces them to village status or even an abandoned site. In Anglo-Saxon Somerset we have instead a situation where limited evidence shows places displaying some urban characteristics at one time but not another. Subsequently, marginal places seem to be towns for a time, then fail but are later revived.

Fluctuations could be due to many causes, ranging from disasters to the trade cycle. Beginning with disasters, these could be natural as with storms, floods or epidemics. We have seen how Watchet suffered from serious storm damage in 1458. Dunster suffered from the more insidious problem of silting. The combined impact was their decline and the rise of Minehead. Equally disasters could be man-made. They could be accidental, as with the fires that periodically afflicted most pre-modern towns. For example Collinson reported major fires at Ilminster in 1491 and Wincanton in 1747 (Collinson 1791 i 2 & iii 31). But the worst examples were the result of war. Thus in 1088 in a short-lived rebellion against William Rufus, one of the chief rebels, Robert de Mowbray, burnt Bath. As a result Bishop John de Villula was able to buy the town and mint from the King. Bath lost the advantages of being a royal borough. The impact of the English Civil War was greater. Virtually all the county's towns suffered but Taunton and Bridgwater were particularly hard hit. The Royalists' desperate attempts to take Taunton before a relief force could arrive failed but left two-thirds of the houses destroyed and most of the others stripped of thatch, which had been fed to the garrison's horses. Conversely, when the Parliamentarians took Bridgwater all Eastover was burnt and there was considerable damage in the main town on the west bank (Underdown 1973 94-5 & 109-10).

Trade cycles are less dramatic but we have seen how fluctuations in the textiles trades had major impacts. The changes in ranking are closely associated with changing demand mainly for different types of woollen cloth but also for gloves, stockings, linen and, at the end of our period, silk. Changes in technology and transport also played their part. The bridge at Bridgwater led inevitably to the decline of Langport which was then accessible only to small craft. Increasing sizes of ship also downgraded many of the smaller ports and anchorages. Similarly changes in fortune in the south of the county reflected variations in the main London to Exeter route and how many of Wincanton, Yeovil, Crewkerne and Chard lay on it at a particular time.

Again the balance with the countryside varied with time. Industry might shift into rural areas to escape restriction. However, this does not seem to have been a major difficulty in Somerset. Towns such as Bruton and Wells seem to have worked harmoniously with surrounding rural producers and to have used appropriate rural sites for activities such as fulling mills. As we have seen in this area the conflict was between Bristol and both the towns and villages of surrounding areas. More important was a loss of status in relative terms from around 1550 as agricultural prices increased. We have noted how this was the period when country gentlemen began to colonise the towns.

There are less quantifiable factors relating to enterprise, initiative and access to capital. In turn enterprising individuals could be affected by the actions of town lords or town authorities. Medieval town founders generally acted for economic motives. Towns returned useful yields in cash and stimulated the economy of surrounding rural areas. Where there were town councils with reasonable powers this were dominated by the town elite so they would have been sympathetic to trade. Things changed in the sixteenth century. As we have seen, the gentry moved into the towns. They were often more interested in 'influence'. Simultaneously the larger towns were losing the small class of merchants that had played a major role in driving their economies. Such persons now operated out of Bristol or even London. There was a major change in the nature of the county's towns. This was worsened by the impact of the Reformation in towns with large religious establishments. Glastonbury lost a resident institution with an income of about £4,000 per annum. The monastic site dwindled to ruins. In 1524-5 the town ranked 85 in the country in terms of assessed wealth. As mentioned when Celia Fiennes passed through, she thought it 'now a poor ragged place' (Morris 1949 242).

Having reviewed the general situation, we must now turn to the specific questions that have been raised beginning with the reasons for the profusion of small towns in Somerset. Inevitable there is again no simple answer but an interplay of factors. Partly it is attributable to the physical nature of the county. Its geology and land forms are varied. This variety in turn gives a large number of resources. In the only other systematic study undertaken in the south-west, Kowaleski examined Devon. She concluded that difficulties of transport and diversity of products created the dense pattern of towns there (Kowaleski 1995 41-80). This reasoning seems applicable to Somerset. Regular catchments such as six and two-thirds or ten mile radiuses around towns do not work if the pattern is interrupted by steep hills or wetlands that were impassable for half the year. More generally this study indicates that too much weight can be given to theoretical catchments and simple hierarchies of towns. Throughout the High Middle Ages and after, Somerset towns operated in a world that extended to Exeter in the west, Bristol in the north and Salisbury and Southampton in the east. Beyond this the presence of London was apparent.

The physical fracturing in Somerset may have contributed to the next important factor. This was a tendency towards administrative division going back to Anglo-Saxon times. The king and the county administration (which was a major part of the apparatus of government at that time) preferred to spread functions around the county. We saw this in the *burh,* palace and minster division at Axbridge, Cheddar and Wells. It is also shown in the profusion of mints. For some reason a wide geographical spread of mint sites was preferred even if it meant that some had to rely on periodic visits by an itinerant moneyer. Possibly this abundance was aided by the large number of royal manors which provided potential locations. But that merely raises yet again the question, why did this occur in Somerset? Neighbouring counties also had many royal manors. In Domesday 35 manors are listed under lands of the king in Somerset. Larger Devon had 72 royal manors, Dorset 31, Gloucestershire 67 (a number inflated as

Tewkesbury Abbey and its estates were in the royal hands in 1086) and Wiltshire only 23. As Wiltshire is closest to Somerset in numbers of *burhs* and mints there is no clear pattern here. However, there is Hill's suggestion which argues for a deliberate policy in Somerset and Wiltshire in reaction to the scale of alienation to the Church (Hill 1978 222).

Possibly parts of the Somerset pattern may have even more ancient roots. The southern part of the county was noted for a profusion of all of Anglo-Saxon mints, early royal manors, small hundreds and medieval towns. Before that it had been characterised by a pattern of Roman roads that converged on Ilchester and a concentration of villas around that town. The two are certainly linked in that the road pattern remained and effected the siting of later towns. In addition it may be that some Roman estates survived as land holdings, passed to the kings of Wessex and served as centres for hundreds, minsters and mints. They were then potential town sites.

Was this already extensive network over-stretched by greedy lords in the period 1100 to 1300? The answer seems to be no. Most lords confined themselves to a single creation and there is, apart from Southwick, no blatantly competitive creation adjoining an established town. This contrasts with the foundation of Bridgetown Pomeroy across the River Dart from Totnes or the plots the lord of Cogges laid out on the east of Whitney (Beresford 1967 116 & 119; Bond and Hunt 1979 24-5). The only landowner who might be suspected of trying rather too hard was the bishop. The bishops' creations comprised a major success at Wells, two places which did not perform well initially but were well established by the sixteenth century, that is Chard and Wellington, Wiveliscombe which was never more than a modest success and three total failures at Southwick, Newport and Rackley. In part this may be explained by the bishops becoming large-scale town founders rather late. Apart from Wells itself and Rackley, their activity is after 1200 when Joscelin had moved the administration back to Wells at about the centre of the county. Previous inaction may reflect a very peripheral position at Bath. Also their strategy for increased wealth was then concentrated in first absorbing the role of abbot of Bath and then under Savaric (1192-1205) that of Glastonbury. However, it is worth noting that other bishops were prone to over-optimistic foundations. The creations of the bishops of Winchester included Newtown near Newbury, ranked by Keene as the least town in the south-east in 1334. Overton was little better and a third of their creations, New Alresford, very modest (*CUH* i 653).

Finally there is the question of the influence of Bristol. Certainly its impact is clear in northern Somerset where fully fledged towns are few and, as we have seen, some services were provided by a network of places that could be described as micro-towns or service villages. It is more difficult to discover whether its influence extended beyond Mendip and kept towns small across the county. The example of Gloucester to the north suggests that it could not have been entirely responsible although it no doubt helped keep places such as Wells small even at the height of their economic success. As explained, Bristol's influence became more intense after 1500.

To sum up, it seems likely that physical circumstances and decisions made before 1066 established a pattern that was so dispersed that it became impossible to accumulate urban functions in a single place so as to ensure its growth. Perhaps it could have been different. If the bishop had been established at Glastonbury and the courts and mint moved there from Ilchester the results might have been a single large town providing all higher level services for the county. As this did not happen the post-Conquest pattern was inevitable. If Hill is right, it did not happen, because the king had a financial interest in a pattern of many towns. If his attractive suggestion is correct, Ethelred II is probably largely responsible for the situation in Somerset. Subsequently, the lords who founded towns did not act with unusual extravagance and the influence of Bristol south of Mendip only helped to confirm the situation.

The other recurring question has been the issue of what makes a town if the place is small and has limited functions. As explained, there is no clear answer. It will depend on how we weight various criteria. Thought is needed as to how conclusive it should be that earlier ages actually regarded a place as a town.

Obviously much of what has been said here is provisional. Information is often scanty except for places which have been scrutinised by researchers for the *Victoria County History*, together with Bath and Wells, which have drawn the attention of considerable numbers of scholars including active local groups. This needs supplementing. There is a clear need for local studies of such places as Wrington and Chew Magna. Thematic studies are also required. Marketing and transport networks are two vital and inter-related areas. Some older work also needs review. It is hoped that this work will encourage more activity.

BIBLIOGRAPHY

Alcock L. 1995 *Cadbury Castle, Somerset: the early medieval archaeology.* University of Wales Press, Cardiff

Angus J. and Vanes J. (eds) 1974 *The Ledger of John Smythe.* Bristol Record Society (Vol. XXVIII) and Royal Commission on Historical Manuscripts (JP19), HMSO, London

Aston M.A. 1984 'The Towns of Somerset' in Haslam 1984

—1985 *Interpreting the Landscape.* Batsford, London

—1993 *Monasteries.* Batsford, London

—2002 'Early Monasteries in Somerset – Models and Agendas' in Ecclestone, Gardner, Holbrook and Smith 2002

Aston M.A. and Burrow I. 1982 *The Archaeology of Somerset.* Somerset County Council

Aston M.A. and Iles R. (eds) 1984 *The Archaeology of Avon.* Avon County Council

Aston M.A. and Leech R.H. 1977 *Historic Towns in Somerset.* Council for Rescue Archaeology in Avon, Gloucestershire and Somerset, Bristol

Aston M.A. and Lewis C. (eds) 1994 *The Medieval Landscape of Wessex.* Oxbow Books, Oxford

Bailey D.S. 1982 *Canonical Houses of Wells.* Alan Sutton, Gloucester

Barry J. 2000 'South-West', *CUH* ii 67-92

Bates E.H. (ed.) 1900 *The Particular Description of Somerset.* Somerset Record Society (Vol. 15), Taunton

Batt M. 1973 'The Burghal Hidage – Axbridge'. *Proceedings of the Somerset Archaeological and Natural History Society* 51, 22-5

Beresford M.W. 1967 *New Towns of the Middle Ages.* Lutterworth, London

Beresford M.W. and Finberg H.P.R. 1973 *English Medieval Boroughs: a Handlist.* David and Charles, Newton Abbot

Bettey J.H. 1986 *Wessex from AD1000.* Longman, London

Biddle M. 1976 'Towns' in Wilson (1976) 99-150

Bond C.J. and Hunt A.M. (eds) 1979 'Recent archaeological work in Pershore' *Vale of Evesham Historical Society Research Paper IV* 1-62

Boone M. and Stabel P. (eds) 2000 *Shaping Urban Identity in Late Medieval Europe.* Garant, Leuven and Apeldoorn

Britnell R.H. 1981 'The proliferation of markets in England' *Economic History Review* 2nd series 34, 209-21

Bunyard B.D.M. (ed.) 1941 *The Brokerage Book of Southampton 1439-40.* Southampton Record Society

Bush R.J. 1975 *The Book of Taunton.* Barracuda, London

Bush R.J. and Aston M.A. 1984 'The Town: History and Topography' in Leach (1984)

Camden W. 1971 *Britannia.* David and Charles Reprints, Newton Abbot

Carus-Wilson E.M. (ed.) 1937 *The Overseas Trade of Bristol in the Later Middle Ages.* Bristol Record Society (Vol. 7), Bristol, 1937

Chandler J. (ed.) 1993 *John Leland's Itinerary*. Alan Sutton, Stroud

Clark P. 2000 'Small Towns 1750-1840' *CUH* ii 733-73

Clark P., Gaskin K. and Wilson A. 1989 *Population Estimates of English Small Towns 1550-1851*. Centre for Urban History, Leicester University, Working Paper 3, Leicester

Colby F.J. (ed.) 1876 *The Visitation of Somerset 1623*. Harleian Society (Vol. xi), London

Colchester L.S (ed.) 1984 *Wells Cathedral Communar's Accounts 1327-1600*. Friends of Wells Cathedral, Wells

—(ed.) 1988 *Wells Cathedral Escheator's Accounts 1369-1600* 2 vols, privately, Wells

Collinson J. 1791 *The History and Antiquities of the County of Somerset* 3 vols Cruttwell, Bath.

Corbett W.J. 1926 'The development of the duchy of Normandy and the Norman Conquest of England' *Cambridge Medieval History*. Cambridge University Press v 505-13

—1992 *The Origins of Somerset*. Manchester University Press

Coster M. 1984 'Late Saxon Avon' in Aston and Iles 1984, 83-94

Cunliffe B. 1984 'Bath: retrospect and prospect' in Aston and Iles 1984, 161-72

—1986 *The City of Bath*. Alan Sutton, Gloucestershire

Defoe D. 1948 *A Tour Through England and Wales* 2 vols, Everyman, London

Dickinson F.H. (ed.) 1899 *Kirby's Quest for Somerset, etc*. Somerset Record Society (Vol. 3), Taunton

Dolley R.H.M. and Metcalfe D.M. 'The Reform of the English Coinage under Eadgar' in Dolley R.H.M. (ed.) *Anglo-Saxon Coins*. London, 1961

Drage C. 1987 'Urban Castles' in Schofield and Leech 1987

Dunning R.W. 1974 'Somerset towns in the fourteenth century' *Notes and Queries for Somerset and Dorset* xxix, 10-3.

—1983 *A History of Somerset*. Phillimore, Chichester

—1992 *Bridgwater: a History and Guide*. Alan Sutton, Stroud

Dyer A. 1991 *Decline and Growth in English Towns 1400-1640*. Macmillan, London

—2000a 'Ranking Lists of English Medieval Towns' *CUH* i, 747-70

—2000b 'Small Market Towns' *CUH* ii 425-59

Dyer C. 1989 'The consumer and the market in the later middle ages' *Economic History Review* 2nd series 42, 305-27

—1998 'Trade, towns and the church: ecclesiastical consumers in the urban economy of the West Midlands 1290-1540' in Slater and Rosser 1998, 55-75

—2000a 'Smaller Towns 1270-1540' *CUH* i 505-37

—2000b *Bromsgrove: a small town in Worcestershire in the Middle Ages*. Worcestershire Historical Society, Occasional Publication 9, Worcester

Ecclestone M., Gardner K.S., Holbrook N. and Smith A. (eds) 2002 *The Land of the Dobunni*. Committee for Archaeology in Gloucestershire and Council for British Archaeology (South West), Gloucester

Eld F.J. (ed.) 1895 *Lay Subsidy Roll for the County of Worcester I Edward III*. Worcestershire Historical Society, Worcester

Eliassen F.E. and Erslund G.A. (eds) 1996 *Power, Profit and Urban Land*. Scolar Press, Aldershot

Everitt A. 1967 'The Marketing of Agricultural Produce' *Agrarian History of England and Wales Vol. 4 1500-1640*. Cambridge University Press 466-592

Fawcett T. and Inskip M. 1994 'The making of the Orange Grove' in Fawcett T. (ed.) *Bath History 5*, Millstream Books, Bath

Fry G.S. 1897 'A list of Somerset Recusants' *Notes and Queries for Somerset and Dorset* v 112-21

Glasscock R.E. (ed.) 1975 *The Lay Subsidy of 1334*. British Academy, Records of Social and Economic History, new series 2, London

Green E. (ed.) 1888 *Colleges, Chantries, etc in Somerset in 1548*. Somerset Record Society (Vol. 2), Taunton

—1889a 'A Bath Poll Tax 2 Richard II' *Proceedings of the Bath Natural History and Antiquarian Field Club* 6 (3) 294-315

—1889b 'Bath Lay Subsidies Henry IV to Henry VIII' *Proceedings of the Bath Natural History and Antiquarian Field Club* 6(4) 379-411

—1904 *Certificates of Muster 1569*. Somerset Record Society (Vol. 20), Taunton

Grinsell L. 1984 'The mints of Bath and Bristol' in Aston and Iles 1984, 173-6

Hadwin J.F. 1983 'The medieval lay subsidies and economic history' *Economic History Review* 2nd series, 36

Hall T. 2000 *Minster Churches in the Dorset Landscape*. British series 304, British Archaeological Reports, Oxford.

—2002 'The Reformation of the British Church in the West Country in the 7th Century' in Ecclestone. Gardner, Holbrook and Smith 2002.

Hancock F. 1903 *Minehead*. Barnicott and Pearce, Taunton

—1911 *Wifela's Combe*. Barnicott and Pearce, Taunton

Harvey J.H. (ed.) 1969 *William Worcestre: Itineraries*. Clarendon Press, Oxford

Hase P.H. 1994 'The Church in the Wessex Heartlands' in Aston and Lewis 1994

Haslam J. (ed.) 1984 *Anglo-Saxon Towns in Southern England*. Phillimore, Chichester

Hasler J. and Luker B. 1997 *The Parish of Wookey; a New History*. Wookey Local History Group

Heighway C. 1987 *Anglo-Saxon Gloucestershire*. Alan Sutton, Gloucestershire

Hembry P.M. 1967 *The Bishops of Bath and Wells 1540-1640*. Athlone Press, London

Herbert N.M. (ed.) (1988) *The Victoria County History of Gloucestershire Vol IV Gloucester*. Oxford University Press

Hill D. 1978 *Ethelred the Unready*. British Archaeological Reports, British series 59, Oxford

—1981 *An Atlas of Anglo-Saxon England*. Oxford University Press (2nd edition 1984)

Hill D. and Rumble A.R. 1996 *The Defence of Wessex: The Burghal Hidage and Anglo-Saxon Forts*. Manchester University Press

Hobhouse E. (ed.) 1934 *The Diary of a West Country Physician 1684-1726*. Simpkin Marshall, London

Holdsworth C. 1995 'Bishoprics, Monasteries and the Landscape c. AD 600-1066' in Hooke and Burnell 1995, 27-50

Hooke D. and Burnell S. 1995 *Landscape and Settlement in Britain AD 400-1066*. University of Exeter Press

Hoskins W.G. 1976 *The Age of Plunder*. Longman, London

Howard A.J. (trans.) and Stoate T.L. (ed.) 1975 *The Somerset Protestation Returns and Lay Subsidy rolls 1641-2*. Privately, Almondsbury

Hulbert N.F. 1936 'A Survey of Somerset Fairs' *Proceedings of the Somerset Archaeology and Natural History Society* 82, 87-117

Hunt T.J. (ed.) 1962 *Customs of the manors of Taunton*. Somerset Record Society (Vol. 66), Taunton

Hunt W. (ed.) 1893 *Two Cartularies of Bath Abbey* (2 vols). Somerset Record Society (Vol. 7), Taunton

Keene D. 2000 'The South-east of England'. *CUH* i 545-82

Kemp E.R. and Shorrocks D.M.M. (eds) 1974 *Medieval Deeds of Bath and District*. Somerset Record Society (Vol. 73), Taunton

Kermode J. 2000 'The Greater Towns 1300-1540'. *CUH* i 441-65

Kowaleski M. 1995 *Local Markets and Regional Trade in Medieval Exeter*. Cambridge University Press

—2000 'Port Towns: England and Wales 1300-1540'. *CUH* i 467-94

Leach P. (ed.) 1984 *The Archaeology of Taunton*. Alan Sutton, Gloucestershire

Leach P. and Dunning R.D. 1990 *Ilchester*. Somerset County Council, Taunton

Leech R.H. 1975 *Small Medieval Towns in Avon*. Council for Rescue Archaeology in Avon, Gloucestershire and Somerset, Bristol

Metcalf D.M. 1998 *An Atlas of Anglo-Saxon and Norman Coin Finds c.973-1086*. Royal Numismatic Society and Ashmolean Museum, London

Morris C. (ed.) 1949 *The Journeys of Celia Fiennes*. Cresset Press, London

Nott A. and Hasler J. (eds) 2004 *Wells Convocation Act Books 1589-1665*. Somerset Record Society (Vols 90 and 91), Taunton

Palliser D.M. 1979 *Tudor York*. Oxford University Press

Petruccioli A., Stella M. and Strappa G. (eds) 2003 *The Planned City*. Uniongrafica Corcelli Editrice, Bari

Pevsner N. 1958a *The Buildings of England: North Somerset and Bristol*. Penguin, Harmondsworth.

—1958b *The Buildings of England: South and West Somerset*. Penguin, Harmondsworth

Ponsford M. 1984 'Bristol' in Aston and Iles 1984, 145-60

Ponting K.G. 1957 *The West of England Cloth Industry*. Macdonald, London

Pooley C. 1877 *The Old Stone Crosses of Somerset*. Longmans Green, London

Poyntz Wright P. 1981 *The Parish Church Towers of Somerset*. Avebury

Phythian-Adams C. 1977 'Jolly Cities: Goodly Towns. The current search for England's urban roots' *Urban History Yearbook* 36-9

—1979 *Desolation of a City* Cambridge University Press

Reid R.D. and Scrase A.J. 1981 'A Great House and Two Lanes at Wells' *Proceedings of the Somerset Archaeological and Natural History Society* 125, 31-41

Reynolds S. 1992 'The writing of medieval urban history in England'. *Theoretische Geschiedenis* 19, 49-50

Rodwell W. 2001 *Wells Cathedral: Excavations and Structural Studies 1978-93*. English Heritage

Roskell J.S., Clark L. and Rawncliffe C. 1993 *The History of Parliament: the House of Commons 1386-1421*. Alan Sutton, Stroud

Russell J.C. 1948 *British Medieval Population*. University of New Mexico Press, Albuquerque (facsimile from Ann Arbor, Michigan and London 1981)

Schofield J. and Leech R.H. (eds) 1987 *Urban Archaeology in Britain*. Research Report 61, Council for British Archaeology, York

Scrase A.J. 1984 'Wells Inns' *Notes and Queries for Somerset and Dorset* xxxi 378-95

—1989a *Wells: a Study of Town Origins and Early Development*. UWE, Bristol

—1989b 'A French Merchant in Fourteenth Century Wells' *Proceedings of the Somerset Archaeology and Natural History Society* 133, 131-40

—1989c 'Wells Almshouse Records and topographic reconstruction at Wells' *Notes and Queries for Somerset and Dorset* xxxii 738-48

—1989d 'Development and change in burgage plots: the example of Wells' *Journal of Historical Geography* 15(4) 349-65

—1989/90 'What's in a name – the inhabitants of Wells c.1215 to 1350' *Report of the Wells Natural History and Archaeological Society,* 101 & 2, 26-40

—1993 *Wells: the Anatomy of a Medieval and Early Modern Property Market.* UWE, Bristol

—1999 *Streets and Market Places in Southwest England: encroachments and improvements.* Edwin Mellen Press, Lampeter

—2000 'Crosses, Conduits and other street furniture in the South West of England' in Boone and Stabel 2000, 201-19

—2002a 'The citizens of medieval Wells' *History Round Wells* 6, 35-46

—2002b *Medieval Town Planning: a modern invention?.* UWE, Bristol

Scrase A.J. and Hasler J. 2002 *Wells Corporation Properties.* Somerset Record Society (Vol. 87), Taunton

Shaw D.G. 1993 *The Creation of a Community.* Clarendon Press, Oxford

Shilton D. and Holworthy R. (eds) 1932 *Wells City Charters.* Somerset Record Society (Vol. 46) Taunton

Slater T.R. 1996 'Medieval town-founding on English Benedictine estates' in Eliassen and Erslund 1996 70-92

—2000 'The South-West of England' *CUH* i 583-607

—2003 'Planning English Medieval Street Towns' in Petruccioli A., Stella M. and Strappa G. (2003) 176-181

Slater T.R. and Rosser G. 1998 *The Church in the Medieval Town.* Ashgate, Aldershot

Smith B. and Ralph E. 1972 *A History of Bristol and Gloucestershire.* Darwin Finlayson, Beaconsfield

Steane J.M. 1984 *The Archaeology of Medieval England and Wales.* Croom Helm, London

Stevens Cox J. 1952 *The Ancient Churches of Ilchester.* Privately, Ilchester

Torr V.J. 1980 'Ecclesiastical Somerset in 1563' *Notes and Queries for Somerset and Dorset* xxx 83-94.

Toulmin Smith L. (ed.) 1964 *Leland's Itinerary in England and Wales.* Centaur Press, London, 5 volumes (originally published 1906-10 by Bell)

Trent C. and Trent F. (eds) 1980 *Domesday Book: Somerset.* Phillimore, Chichester

Underdown D. 1973 *Somerset in the Civil War and Interregnum.* David and Charles, Newton Abbot

Weaver F.W. (ed.) 1885 *Visitations of Somerset 1531 and 1573.* Privately, Exeter

—(ed.) 1905 *Somerset Medieval Wills (1531-58).* Somerset Record Society (Vol. 21) Taunton

Webb A.J. (ed.) 2002 *Two Tudor Subsidy Assessments for the County of Somerset 1558 and 1581-2.* Somerset Record Society (Vol. 88), Taunton

Wheeler A. 1984 'Fishbones' in Leach 1984, 193-4

Wilson D.M. (ed.) 1976 *The Archaeology of Anglo-Saxon England.* Methuen, London

Wood F.A. (1903) *Collections for a Parochial History of Chew Magna.* Privately, Bristol

Woodward G.H. (ed.) 1982 *Chantry Grants.* Somerset Record Society (Vol. 77), Taunton

INDEX